Diesels Nationwide

Class 55 No. 9006 *The Fife & Forfar Yeomanry* takes
an air-conditioned train up Holloway bank at the start of
its journey north from the capital.

DIESELS NATIONWIDE

by Keith Montague

Oxford Publishing Co.

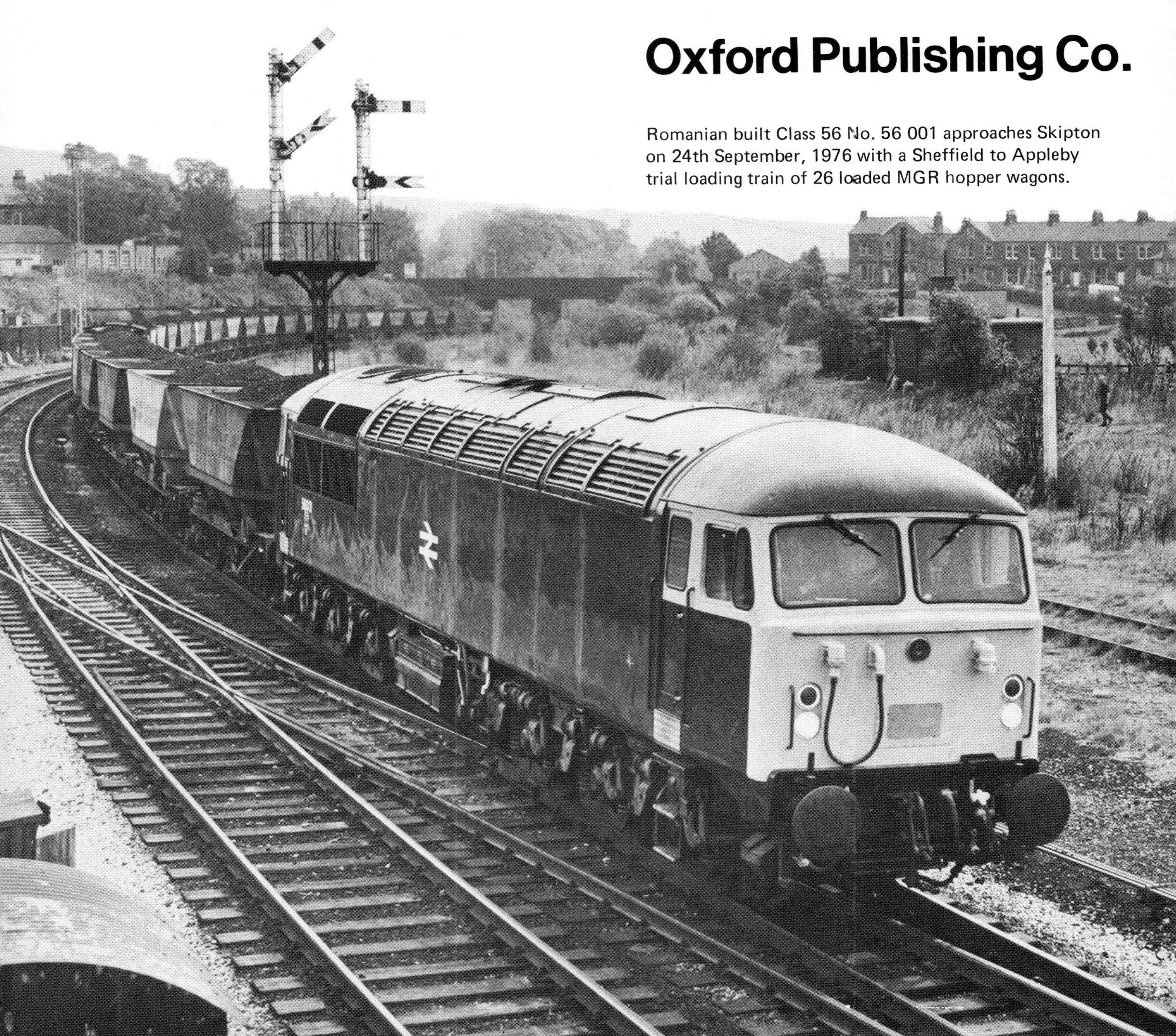

Romanian built Class 56 No. 56 001 approaches Skipton on 24th September, 1976 with a Sheffield to Appleby trial loading train of 26 loaded MGR hopper wagons.

Printed by Blackwell's
in the City of Oxford
Typesetting by Gem Graphic Services, Didcot, Oxon.
Published by Oxford Publishing Co., 8 The Roundway,
Headington, Oxford.

Acknowledgements

I should like to thank D. Akrigg, H.J. Ashman, F.R.P.S.,
British Rail, Commercial Photographers Newbury,
R. Coffin, G. Dowling, M. Earley, J. Eden, D. Ewart,
G. Hounsell, B. Jackson, R. Kennedy, J. Lean, B. Morrison,
G.W. Morrison, B. Nicolle, N. Preedy, S. Rickard,
G. Scott-Lowe, P. Waylett, J. Whiteley and M.J. Woodward
for their valuable assistance in making photographs
available and providing information on the identification
of locations etc. on some of the pictures.

An unusual visitor to Kings Cross in the form of No.
46 030 seen taking empty stock to Finsbury Park on
12th June, 1975.

Introduction

In this, my third album dedicated to diesel trains, I have attempted an expansion of the theme of 'Diesels — Western Style' and 'Westerns, Hymeks and Warships'. These previous volumes, which have proved very popular, highlighted the Western Region's unique hydraulic transmission locomotives and I feel there is now a need to give nationwide coverage to the many different types of diesel locomotives built to work in this country.

The prelude to the British diesel era actually started as long ago as the 1930's when the then London Midland & Scottish Railway experimented with 0-6-0 diesel shunters and found that they tended to be superior in many ways to steam locomotives. The trend was followed by other railway companies and many features of these pioneers were to eventually be incorporated in the standard British Railways shunter whose numbers are now legion.

The LM&SR also pioneered main-line diesel traction when it introduced Co-Co 1600 hp diesel-electric locomotive No. 10000 in 1947, heralding the dawn of the diesel era in Britain. Sister engine No. 10001 followed in 1948 under British Railway auspices and in 1951 the Southern Region built three more main-line diesel electric locomotives at Ashford Works. Steam, of course, still reigned supreme and the enthusiasts of the day, watching the new diesels in action on such trains as 'The Royal Scot' and the 'Atlantic Coast Express', little appreciated that this was a start of things to come.

The main impetus to dieselisation came in 1955 with the announcement of the British Railways modernisation plan. Along with proposals for colour light signalling, power signal boxes and continuous fitted braking for all freight vehicles, this sweeping scheme envisaged the elimination of steam locomotives by the mid 1970's and their replacement by diesel traction as an interim measure to complete electrification. The idea seemed unbelievable, but diesel was in fact to oust steam completely (except for the Vale of Rheidol line) by 1968.

Among the priorities of the plan was the replacement of the traditional steam hauled branch trains by diesel multiple units, an idea which had been tried successfully by the former Great Western Railway. To this end a variety of units were ordered from private companies or built by British Railways, mainly with mechanical transmissions.

In 1956 the first of these trains were put to work on former Great Eastern branch lines in Norfolk and Suffolk, where they at once found favour with the travelling public. They were cleaner, more comfortable and afforded passengers a hitherto unseen view of the 'road' ahead. Diesel multiple units cut costs and improved operating efficiency on many branch lines, but they were too late to save some of the little-used but picturesque lines which were closing around this time.

In 1957, a start was made on the main line dieselisation programme. A batch of Type 2 diesel electric locomotives were ordered from the Brush Traction Company to replace steam on the main lines of the former Great Eastern Railway. A new maintenance depot was built alongside the old steam shed at Stratford and railway staff attended extensive courses to learn the new skills involved in driving and maintaining the new form of traction. After initial 'teething troubles' these locomotives proved extremely successful and as class 31's, are still giving yeoman service today, ranging far and wide from their native territory.

During the same year, the first of 54 Type 1 Bo-Bo diesel electric locomotives were ntroduced for freight work on the Eastern Region, on the pattern of 'Hood' units of the U.S.A. Built by the British Thomson-Houston Company, this was the first of several non-standard classes ordered from private manufacturers, some of which consisted of as few as ten locomotives.

The Western Region opted for hydraulic transmissions on its diesels and in 1957 the North British Locomotive Company started to build five of the first generation 'Warship' class locomotives — the first being No. D600 *Active* which appeared on prestige Western Region expresses such as the 'Cornish Riviera Limited' and 'The Torbay Express' the following year.

The first of the British Railways built classes, the Sulzer Type 2's made their debut in the same year on passenger and freight workings. Some were allocated to the Southern Region for Dover express duties prior to third rail electrification while others went to Scotland where they gave valuable service.

Pitfalls were encountered from this policy of non-standardisation. Some classes failed to meet expectations in terms of reliability and others were simply not suited to the duties to which they were first allocated, but as design and operating experience built up, the situation improved.

For the enthusiast, there was a fascinating variety of diesel locomotives to be seen, and this in some measure compensated for the gradual disappearance of beloved steam. Many of these classes, including all of the Western Region hydraulics and several prototype locomotives have since passed into oblivion, but lessons learnt from them have resulted in vastly improved efficiency and reliability of the present, more standardised fleet.

The majority of British Rail's current top link diesels such as the numerous Class 45's, 46's and 47's have been built up at British Rail Workshops, but Class 31's, 33's, 37's, 40's and 50's remain as a tribute to private enterprise.

A notable exception to the general rule of standardisation is, of course, the twenty-two English-Electric built Class 55 'Deltic' locomotives of the Eastern Region which after some fifteen years are still the mainstay of the East Coast route Inter-City expresses from Kings Cross.

During the early days of dieselisation, classes tended to keep to their own territories and the appearance of a 'foreign' locomotive was something of an event. Today, with more intensive utilisation of a rationalised fleet, the situation has changed. It is not unusual for Southern Region Class 33's to be seen as far afield as Cambridge or Paignton or for Class 31's to venture to Barnstaple or Penzance.

This integration has in many ways benefited the enthusiast by giving him the opportunity to see more types of locomotive without the need to travel far from home, but what a pity that more diesel locomotives are not named — this would surely stimulate further interest by each engine's individuality.

Despite diesels being introduced as a 'stop-gap' measure to an electrified future, diesel developments are still progressing. A new Class 56 diesel electric locomotive is on the way for freight work and the production series of 125 mph High Speed Trains are already in regular passenger service, so diesel traction will serve us for some time to come!

In this book I have tried to portray something of the fascination and interest of the diesel locomotive from its earliest days with British Railways. Its forms and liveries have altered considerably over the years, but its aesthetic appeal against a national variety of scenic and industrial backcloths remains constant.

Keith Montague June 1977

The Pioneers

Plate 1: Prototype three-car lightweight diesel unit approaching Princes Risborough on a trial run on 20th May, 1952. This unit later found its way onto the now closed Harrow & Wealdstone — Belmont branch, but its activities there were short lived after it became derailed.

Plate 2: Ex Great Western Railway railcar No. W26 complete with trailer enters Leamington Spa station on a local service from Stratford upon Avon on 25th August, 1952.

Plate 3: Diesel Electric Co-Co locomotive No. 10001 stands outside Brighton works on 2nd October, 1954, six years after making its debut on the main line.

Plate 4: Locomotive No. 10000 was built by the London Midland & Scottish Railway at Derby in 1947 and was the first main line diesel locomotive in this country. This picture shows the engine hard at work with the 13.43 Wolverhampton to Euston express near Watford on 6th July, 1959 (see also photo 3).

Plate 5: Southern Region diesel electric locomotive No. 10201 heads the 13.00 Waterloo to Plymouth express under the Battledown Flyover, west of Basingstoke on 8th September, 1952.

Plate 6: Diesel-electric locomotive No. 10203, built in 1954 by the Southern Region at Ashford heads a Euston bound express near Kenton on 22nd May, 1957. The d.c. electrified local lines to Watford can be seen on the left of the picture.

Plate 7: Having just emerged from Eastleigh Works, the third of the Southern Region main line diesel electric 1 Co-Co 1 locomotives No. 10203, is put on show to the public at the exhibition held at Willesden in June, 1954.

Plate 8: Another shot of No. 10201 on the 13.00 Waterloo — Plymouth train, this time snaking away from the platform at Salisbury station with twelve well laden coaches on 2nd July, 1954.

DP2

Plate 9: English Electric Co-Co type 4 prototype No. DP2 stands at Liverpool (Lime Street) station in June, 1962, whilst a Jinty 0-6-0 tank engine, probably on station pilot duties, manages to get its smokebox into the picture.

Plate 10: A month later the same locomotive is seen approaching the capital with the 14.05 express from Liverpool (Lime Street).

Experimental 'FALCON'

The *Falcon* emblem and nameboard.

Plate 11: The prototype Brush Class 53 diesel electric locomotive No. 1200 *Falcon* awaits departure from No. 1 platform at Paddington on 9th September, 1971 with a Bristol bound train. A Class 52 diesel hydraulic locomotive stands at the head of another service on the adjoining platform. *Falcon* was built as an experimental engine in 1961 and has been used for both passenger and freight work during its varied career which ended in 1976 when it was finally withdrawn from traffic.

Shunters Galore!

Plate 12: Diesel electric 0-6-0 locomotive No. 15203, built by the Southern Railway in 1937 at Ashford, pictured on freight marshalling duties at Norwood Junction on 6th November, 1954.

Plate 13: Willesden depot on 20th March, 1955 with diesel electric 0-6-0 No. 12055 resting between duties. Steam locomotives are just visible on the other side of the roadway.

Plate 14: Fowler diesel mechanical 0-4-0 No. ED1 introduced by the London Midland & Scottish Railway as early as 1936, on shed at Patricroft on 23rd August, 1955, alongside a big brother of the steam world!

Plate 15: Diesel electric 0-6-0 No. 15103 at Old Oak Common on 21st November, 1954. This locomotive was introduced by the Great Western Railway and although in British Railways ownership, still sports a cast side number plate.

Plate 16: Ruston and Hornsby diesel electric 0-6-0 No. PWM 650 outside Swindon Works on 6th November, 1955, just two years after this type of engine was first introduced to British Railways.

Plate 17: Diesel electric 0-6-0 No. 13013 takes a rest between duties outside Eastleigh shed on 2nd July, 1954.

Plate 18: Diesel mechanical 0-6-0 No. 11109 awaits work at Kings Cross shed on 8th May, 1955.

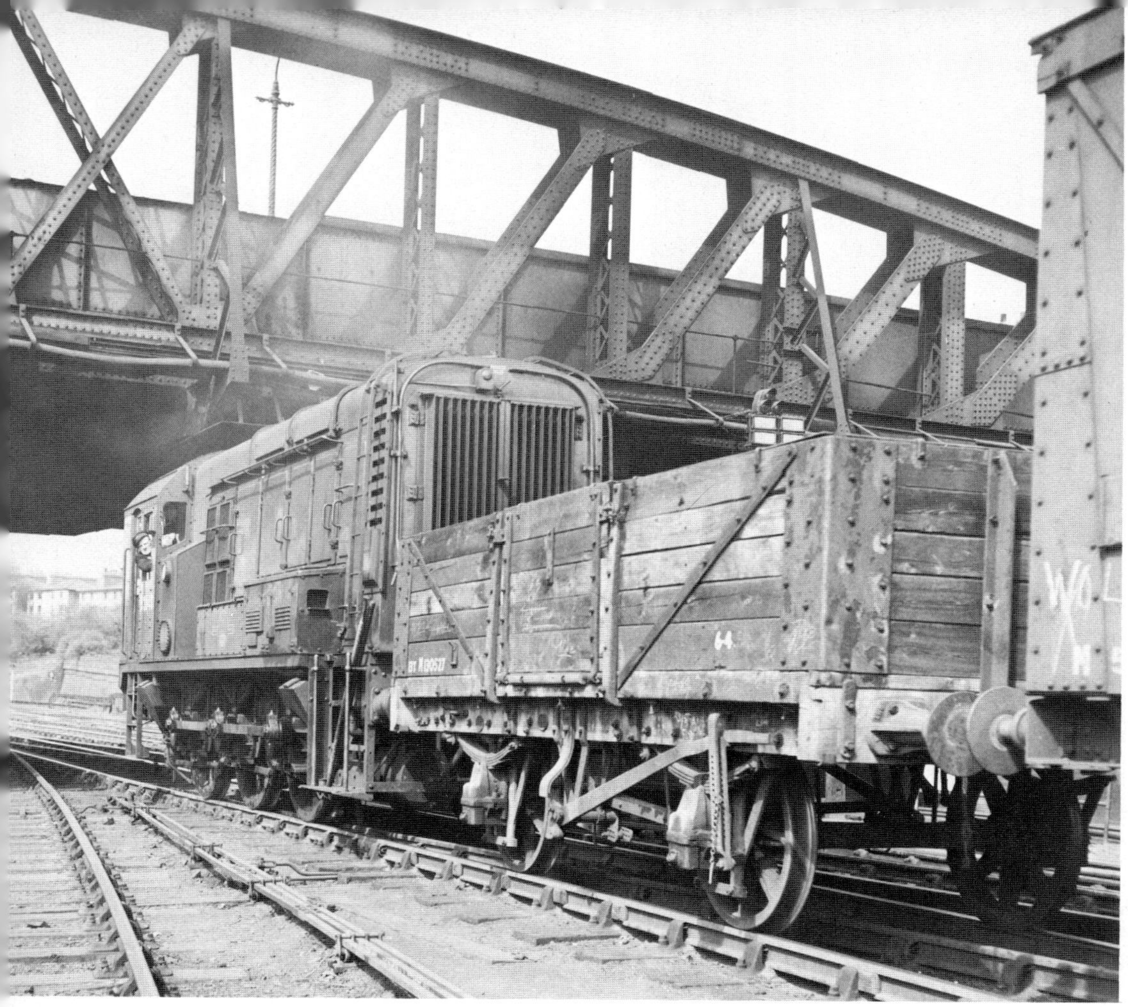

Plate 19: Undoubtedly the most successful type of shunting engine in service on British Rail — the Class 08 diesel electric locomotives. These 250 bhp units were introduced in 1953 and have two English Electric nose-suspended traction motors and double reduction gear drive. This picture shows No. D 3849, since renumbered 08 682 hard at work on Camden bank in April, 1960.

Plate 20: No. D 3847 (now 08 680) marshalls up the wagons in busy Camden yard in April, 1960.

Plate 21: The end of the line — condemned Class 03 diesel mechanical 0-6-0 shunters No's. 03 099, 03 068, 03 076, 03 153 and 03 010 stand outside Thornaby diesel depot on 22nd April, 1976, awaiting disposal to scrap merchants.

Plate 22: Diesel mechanical 0-6-0 shunter No. 03 142 takes a break from work at Landore. It is interesting to note that this is one of the eight locomotives with cut-down cabs for working on the Burry Port and Gwendraeth Valley line, which has a number of very low bridges on its route.

Plate 23: Ruston and Hornsby Class 07 0-6-0 shunters No's. 07 002 and 07 001 stand in line between duties in Southampton Docks on 13th June, 1976.

Plate 24: Class 02 No. 02 003 at its home maintenance depot, Allerton, on 26th April, 1975. Sadly this class of engine finally became extinct on 1st June, 1975 when No's. 02 001 (then in store) and 02 003 and 02 004 were withdrawn and condemned.

Plate 25: Class 09 0-6-0 No. 4107 busy marshalling tank wagons in Chart Leacon Yards, Ashford, Kent on 5th September, 1973.

Plate 26: No. D 9511 on shunting duties at Llandilo Junction on 1st October, 1964.

Plate 27: Diesel electric 0-6-0 No. 12134 busy shunting an assortment of wagons at Temple Mills Yards, Stratford on 10th April, 1954.

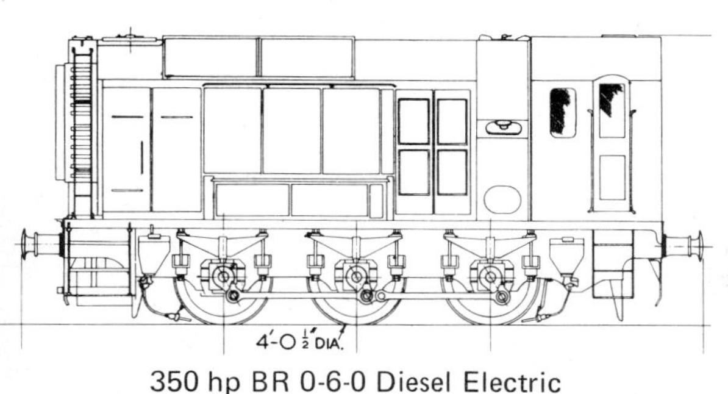

350 hp BR 0-6-0 Diesel Electric

Plate 28: A Clayton Type 1 Bo-Bo diesel stands outside Eastfield shed, Glasgow, in July, 1968.

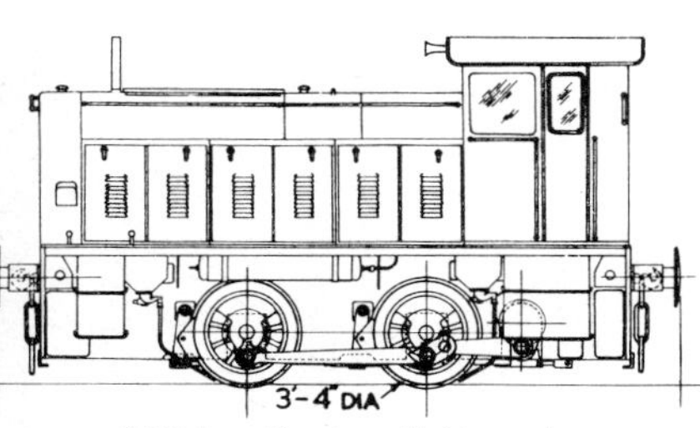

150 hp Ruston & Hornsby

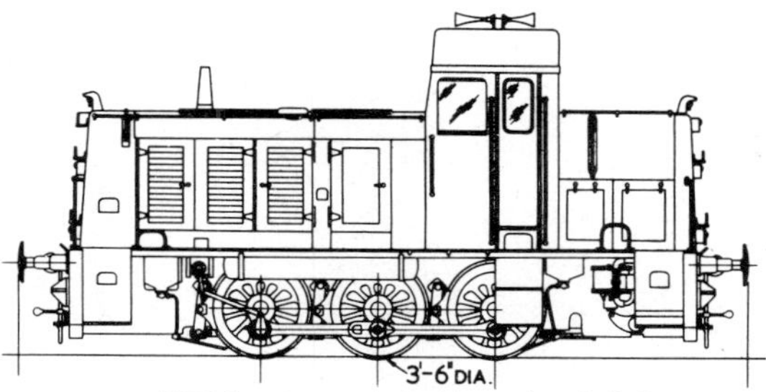

275 hp Ruston & Hornsby 0-6-0

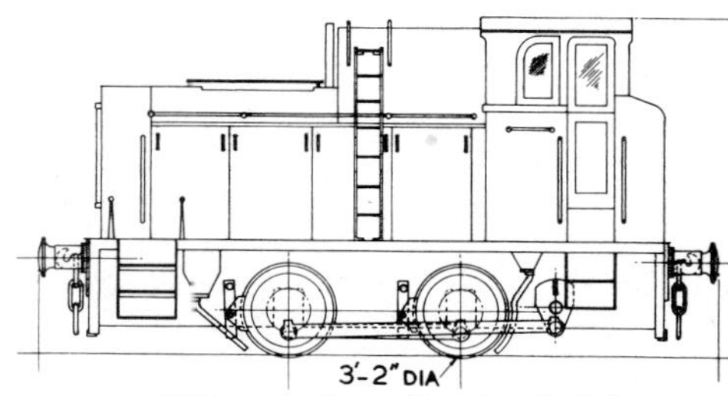

150 hp Andrew Barclay 0-4-0

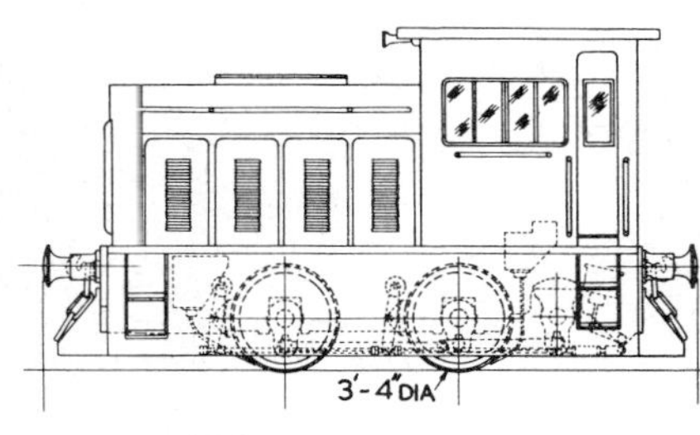

150 hp Hunslet 0-4-0

Plate 29: Rather unusual motive power on a passenger train. An 0-6-0 diesel mechanical shunter, No. D 2029 heads a Kings Cross suburban set of coaches which formed the Saturdays only Henlow Camp leave train on 3rd October, 1959 between Henlow Camp and Shefford.

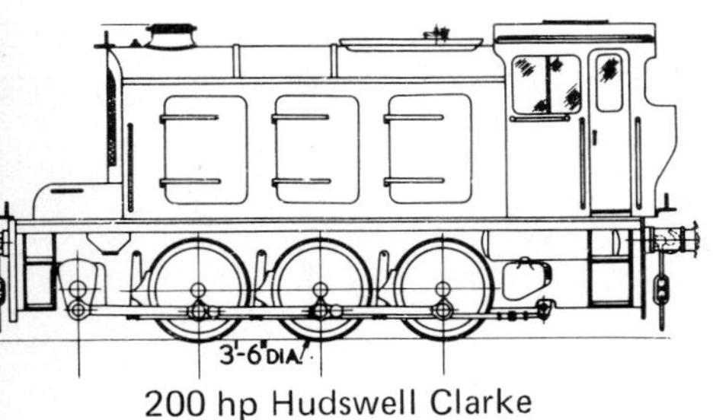

200 hp Hudswell Clarke

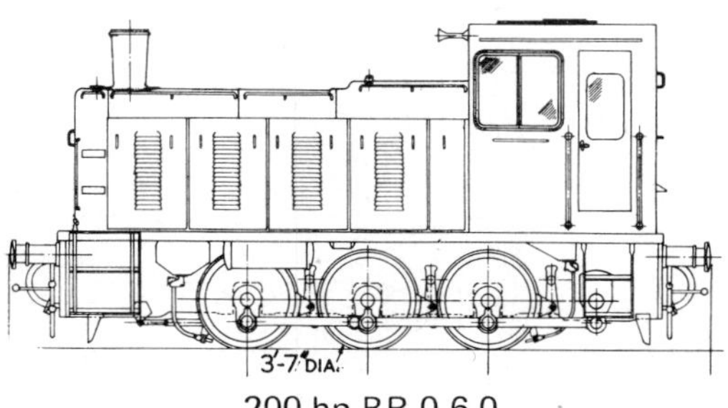

200 hp BR 0-6-0

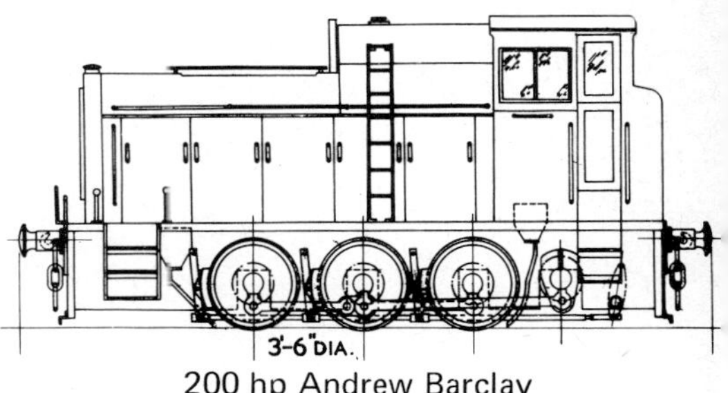

200 hp Andrew Barclay

Plate 30: A study of the nose and tail portions of two Ruston and Hornsby dual braked Class 07 0-6-0 shunters at Southampton Docks. On the left is No. 07 009 and on the right No. 07 001. The remaining engines in this class are all allocated to Eastleigh for use in the docks and the British Rail Engineering Ltd, Works.

Plate 31: Barclay diesel mechanical Class 06 0-4-0 shunter No. 2423 at work with steam crane RS 1074/30 at Aberdeen Ferryhill on 21st March, 1974.

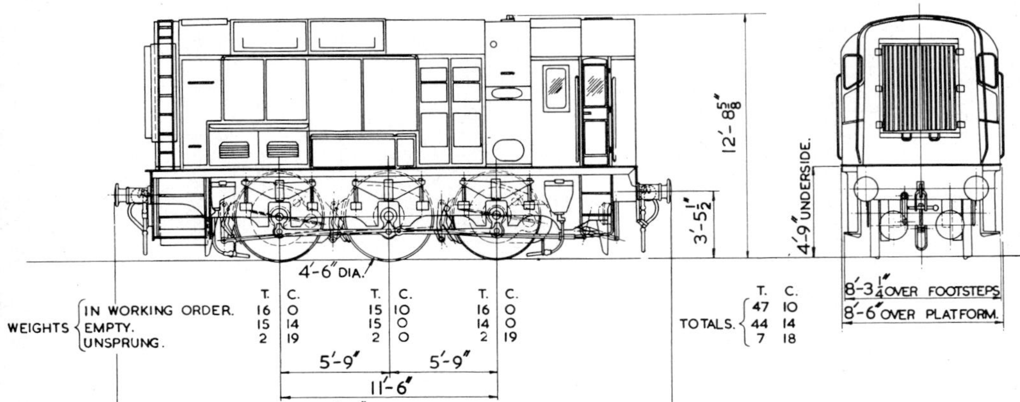

Plate 32: This scenic photograph was taken on 7th July, 1976 at Penzance, with the station pilot 0-6-0 No. 08 840 busily clearing platforms of parcel and newspaper vans to make way for the extra summer trains bringing in many visitors. The familiar shape of St Michael's Mount can be seen in the background.

Plate 33: Barclay diesel mechanical Class 06 0-4-0 shunter No. 06 001 seen at Eastfield. This particular locomotive is at present in store but all the working engines of the class are used exclusively on the Scottish Region in small exchange sidings and in works.

Plate 34: Class 03 shunter No. D 2028 shunts empty stock at Cambridge on 5th September, 1959. Among the steam engines 'on shed' are some vintage GER locomotives, the most prominent being 2-4-0 No. 62785.

Plate 35: A Weymouth Quay train moves cautiously through the town's streets behind a Class 03 shunter in March, 1969. Equipped with a warning bell, the locomotive is escorted by two railwaymen who often have to clear parked cars from the line. In recent years Class 33s have displaced the shunters on these duties.

Plate 36: Yorkshire Engine Co. Class 02 0-4-0 diesel shunter No. D 2865 stands inside Newton Heath depot in December, 1963. This class of shunter was introduced in 1960 with hydraulic transmission and Rolls Royce three stage torque converters.

Plates 37 and 38: These two pictures were taken in Tinsley Yards, Sheffield on 20th September, 1976 and show the unique Class 13 shunters at work. There are only three of the class, all working at Tinsley on hump shunting duties and have the somewhat remarkable wheel arrangement 0-6-0 + 0-6-0. The permanently coupled unit comprises specially weighted master and slave loco, the latter having its cab removed. All have been converted from 0-6-0 Class 08 shunters.

Plate 39: The Holyhead shunter No. 01 002 at the quarry in July, 1974.

Plate 40: Diesel shunter 0-6-0 No. 09 002 shunting tank wagons at Stewarts Lane on 30th June, 1974.

Plate 41: Diesel mechanical shunter Class 05 No. 2554 works an engineers' train near Ryde St. John's Road on the Isle of Wight during March, 1974. The only British Rail diesel on the Island, it was shipped over in 1966 for engineering and shunting duties on the electrified Ryde to Shanklin line, the tracks of which can be seen on the right. The local nickname for the engine is 'Nuclear Fred'!

GLORY WARSHIP CLASS

The Warships

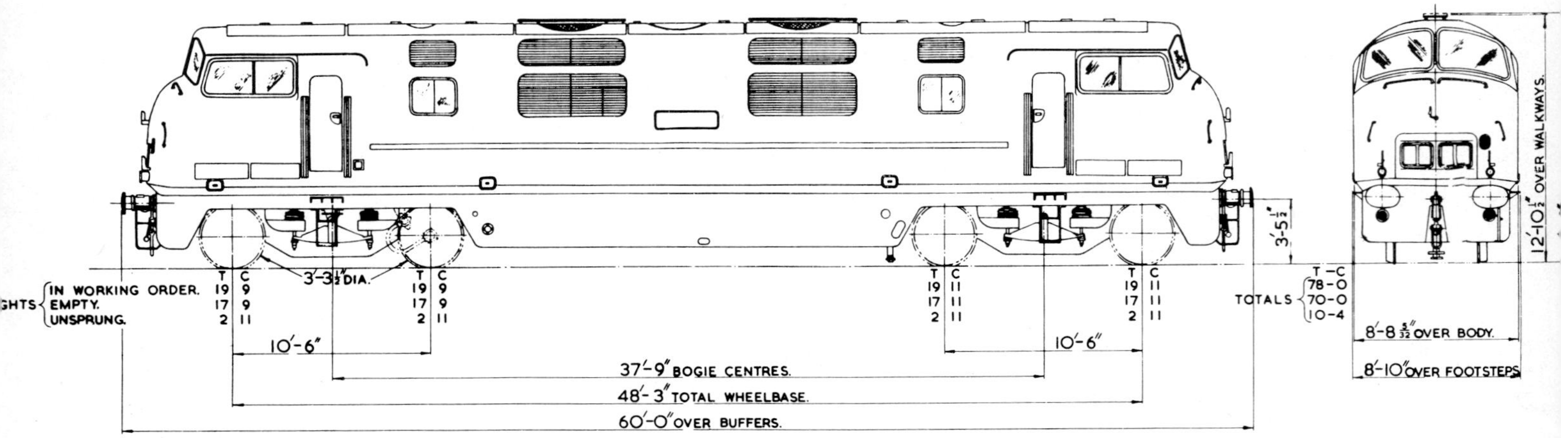

Plate 42: Class 42 No. D 825 *Intrepid* in original 'Warship' green livery, canters through Grateley in July, 1966, with an up Salisbury to Basingstoke local service, comprising an interesting selection of coaching stock. This used to be the junction for the Bulford branch and the picture was taken before Grateley ceased to be a block post. Note the bracket for the branch on the signal post sited at the end of the Down platform.

Plate 43: 'Warship' Class 43 No. 842 *Royal Oak* ventures onto Southern Region electrified lines near Kew with an inter-regional mixed freight working in June, 1971.

Plate 44: No. D 600 *Active* crosses I.K. Brunel's famous Royal Albert Bridge with the 'Cornish Riviera Express', complete with its distinctive headboard. It is single track over the bridge and as can be seen the secondman is about to hand the tablet to the signalman.

Class 24's

Plate 45: Class 24 No. 5052 crosses back to the single line after passing through Towyn on 5th September, 1972 with the 14.06 Tuesdays and Thursdays only freight service from Portmadoc to Shrewsbury.

Plate 46: Class 24 No. 5143 makes ready to depart from Aberystwyth on 4th October, 1973 with a Shrewsbury bound parcels service.

Class 25's

Plate 47: Class 25 No. 25 002 approaches Cove Bay on the outskirts of Aberdeen with a Ferryhill — Dundee mixed freight train.

Plate 48: No's. 25 284 and 25 289 coast through Skipton Station en route to pick up a block train on 8th September, 1976. Note the interesting semaphore signals and tower behind the second locomotive.

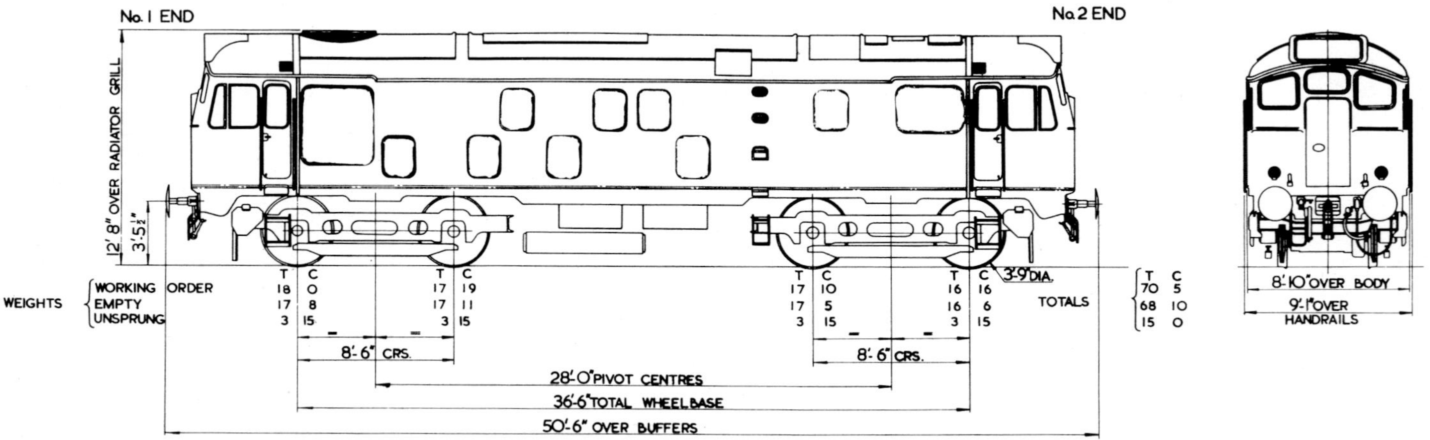

Plate 49: A rural setting on the Scottish East Coast main line at Drumlithie on 28th March, 1974, with Class 25 No. 7581 in charge of an Edinburgh to Aberdeen mixed freight.

Plate 50: No. 25 306 joins the main line just west of Hayle, to go over the viaduct on its way from the Harbour branch to St Erth with a train of empties on 29th July, 1975.

Plate 51: No. 25 268 begins to accelerate through a rather ornate Skipton station on 8th September 1976 with an eastbound pick-up freight train.

Plate 52: A local trip freight from Exmouth to Exeter, headed by No. 25 223, coasts down the steep bank towards Exeter (St. Davids). Note that the distant signal is 'on' and that the train is just about to pass a fixed 10 mph speed restriction.

Tunnels

Plate 53: A Brush Class 47 locomotive heads the Edinburgh portion of a Glasgow/Edinburgh to Birmingham air braked passenger train through Princes Street Gardens towards Carstairs on 21st February, 1975.

Plate 54: Unusual 'Inter City' traction for the St Pancras line in the form of Class 25 No's. 7562 and 5293 at the head of the 15.05 St Pancras to Sheffield service on 16th June, 1973. This photograph shows the train roaring out of the 1058 yard long Elstree tunnel on its journey north.

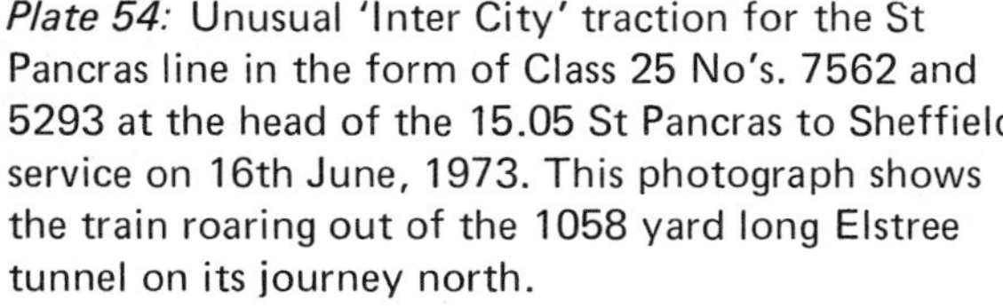

Plate 55: Class 46 No. 46 051 with a mixed freight train about to pass Class 37 No. 37 206 also on freight duties, leaving Newport tunnel on 13th April, 1976.

Plate 56: The 16.05 Kings Cross to Harrogate Inter-City express flashes out of the tunnel and through Hadley Wood station on 8th June, 1974, with Deltic Class 55 No. 55 007 *Pinza* in charge.

Plate 57: Complete with attractive headboard, Class 40 locomotive No. D 324 bursts from the darkness of Kensal Green Tunnel as it leads 'The Caledonian' towards Euston in the early 1960's.

Plate 58: Class 45 No. 45 019 emerges at speed from Elland tunnel on the 11.55 Summer Saturdays only Blackpool to Sheffield train on 21st August, 1976.

Hymeks

Class Details — Hymek

One hundred and one Type 3 Hymek Class 35 locomotives were built by Beyer Peacock for use on the Western Region of British Rail. These diesel-hydraulic 1700 hp B-B locomotives were first introduced in 1961 and weighed 75 tons.

Plate 59: In preparation for construction of an overhead conveyor for the Post Office, station canopies were removed from the east end of all platforms at Bristol (Temple Meads) during June and July, 1970. Hymek Class 35 No. D 7032 stands awaiting the off.

Plate 60: Leaving Paddington, and passing under the road bridges with Royal Oak (London Transport) station on the left, is Hymek No. D 7009 with a train of empty coaching stock for Old Oak Common on 25th April, 1973.

Plate 61: Hymek No. D 7036 in green livery stands on the parcels line between platforms 8 and 9 at Reading General station on 18th July, 1962.

Plate 62: Hymek No. D 7012 passes the rather attractive Radipole Halt, near Weymouth, with a down freight working on 13th August, 1964.

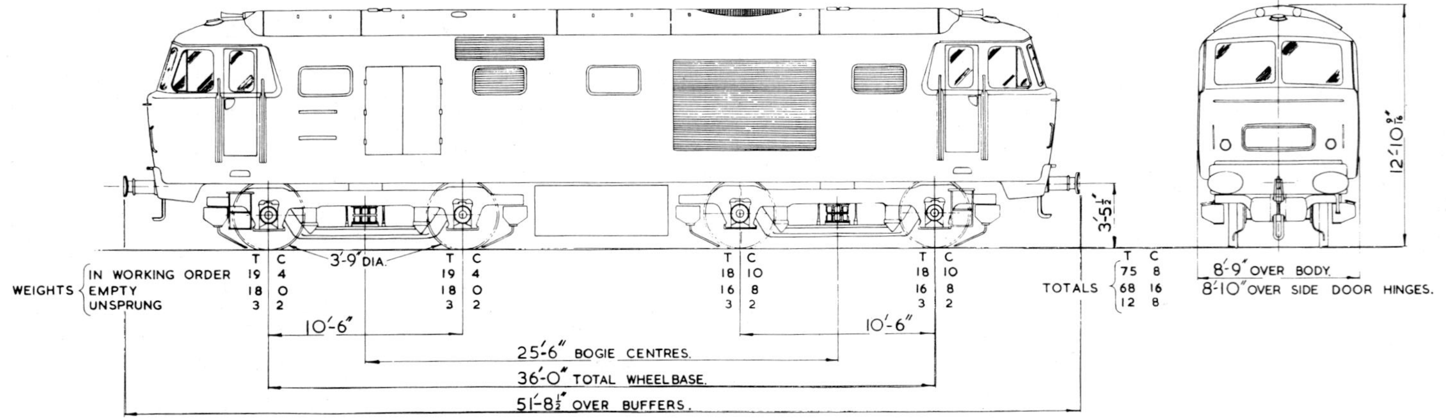

Plate 63: Hymek No. D 7049 trundles an unfitted freight train through the sunshine at Newport in November, 1973.

Plate 64: Night scene at Bristol (Temple Meads) on 14th October, 1972 with part of the station canopies removed. Hymek No. D 7068 stands on the 21.05 for Eastleigh, which terminated short at Westbury on that particular evening due to engineering work.

Plate 65: Weymouth Yard on 22nd April, 1962 with Hymek No's. D 7017 and D 7018 waiting for work. It is interesting to record that No. D 7017 was the last Hymek to have the front yellow panels painted on and No. D 7018 was the first of the class to have them.

Plate 68: The first of the Hymeks, No. D 7000 fitted with miniature snow ploughs, approaching Bath Green Park with a local service from Bristol (Temple Meads) on 5th March, 1966. Sad to relate this line is now closed and the Green Park station site has been taken over by the local corporation.

▶*Plate 66:* The 15.25 Sunday train from Weymouth to Bristol (Temple Meads) takes it easy passing near Upwey and Broadway on 11th August, 1963 with Hymek No. D 7005 in charge.

◀*Plate 67:* Rather an interesting branch line train with green locomotive and maroon coaches — the 11.55 Aberystwyth to Carmarthen service with Hymek No. D 7080 ready to set out from Aberystwyth on 29th May, 1964.

Plate 69: Diesel hydraulic line-up at Old Oak Common depot on 11th October, 1963. From left to right are type 2 No. D 6353, 'Western' type 4 No. D 1000 *Western Enterprise* with raised British Rail emblem, and Hymek type 3 No. D 7065.

Plate 70: A critical eye is cast over Hymek No. D 7025 as it stands at Cardiff with a Swansea to Paddington express in the mid 1960's.

Plate 71: Bristol Zoo is always popular, especially with the children and in 1970 British Rail ran regular excursion trains every Tuesday, Wednesday and Thursday during the school summer holidays from Swansea to Clifton Down — the nearest station to the Zoo. Hymek No. D 7099 is just arriving with the empty stock for the 18.05 from Clifton Down return working on 29th July, 1970.

31's on Parade

Plate 72: Brush Class 31 No's 31 115 and 31 107 pose for the camera at Immingham on 8th September, 1974.

Plate 73: Class 31s seem to have taken over Kings Cross on the morning of 12th June, 1975. The 10.30 local service to Royston is departing behind No. 31 183, whilst No. 31 403 edges out with empty stock for Finsbury Park. Two other Class 31s can be seen on the suburban side of the station. The overall roof in the background of the picture is St. Pancras Station. The ornate tower is part of St. Pancras Chambers, formerly a railway hotel but now used as railway offices.

Plate 74: Kings Cross depot on 28th April, 1974 with several Class 31s including No's. 31 222 and 31 219 waiting for work; a Deltic Class 55 and Brush 47 keep them company.

Plate 75: No. 31 251 pauses in Sheffield Midland station on 7th May, 1974 with 6E 11, a Nottingham to Leeds parcels service.

Plate 76: Engineering operations near Twyford on 28th August, 1976. No 31 260 creeps along the Down Main line whilst unloading of ballast takes place from the 'Dogfish' wagons, especially designed for this purpose.

Plate 77: The High Speed Prototype train made speed trials between London and Bristol in December, 1974 and was authorised to attain speeds of up to 125 mph between Didcot and Challow. On 18th December the prototype is seen on the Down through road at the west end of Bristol (Temple Meads) alongside the more conventional No. 31 242 which had just arrived with 4B05, 05.15 Paddington to Bristol parcels train.

Plate 78: Terraced houses on the outskirts of Harrogate provide the background to No. 31 248 fitted with new marker lights in place of headcode numbers, seen here with an eastbound pick-up freight service.

Plate 79: A long way from home, Finsbury Park based No. 31 174 arrives at Alston sidings to rescue a Metro-Cammell diesel multiple unit which had completely failed whilst working the 14.42 Swindon to Cheltenham service on 5th June, 1976.

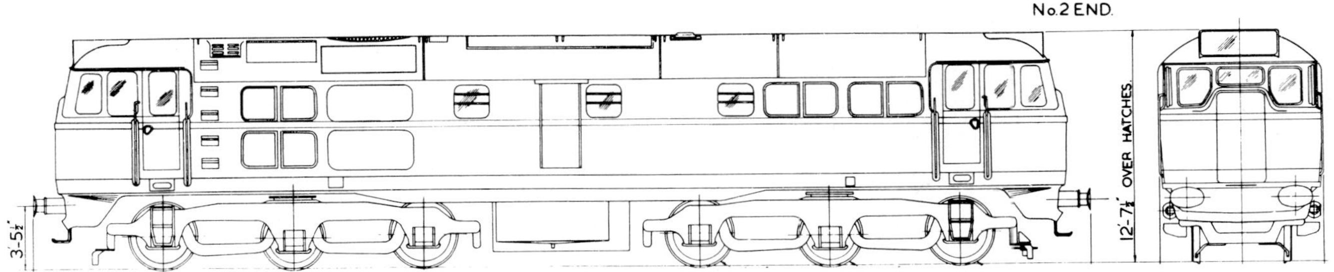

Plate 80: Brush type 2 AIA-AIA, now better known as the Class 31, in mint condition outside Doncaster Works on 23rd May, 1959.

Plate 81: No. 31 107 takes a Sunday break at Immingham depot on 8th September, 1974.

Plate 82: Amidst a conglomeration of overhead power lines, Class 31 No. 5507 approaches Purfleet with a Ripple Lane, Barking to Purfleet trip freight working on 2nd March, 1973.

Big Bridges

Plate 83: In teeming rain a Metro-Cammell three car unit crosses the Tay Bridge with the 09.20 Edinburgh to Dundee service.

Plate 84: The spectacular Forth rail bridge opened in 1890 and is one of the more renowned feats of railway engineering. This picture was taken from South Queensferry on 29th May, 1976 and features two Class 26 locomotives No's. 26 010 and 26 045 double-heading the 08.15 Inverness to Edinburgh passenger train.

Plate 85: The Royal Albert bridge at Saltash was I. K. Brunel's masterpiece in bridging and the portals still proclaim his name, together with the year of the opening of the bridge, 1859. The two main spans are 455 feet each and the bridge is much the same now as when it was built. This photograph was taken on 19th September, 1974 and shows English Electric Class 50 No. 50.030 with the 11.00 Plymouth to Penzance passenger train.

Westerns

Plate 86: An unidentified 'Western' Class 52 locomotive heads the 10.30 Newquay to Paddington summer Saturdays only train, through picturesque countryside between Luxulyan and St. Blazey on the single track Newquay branch on 3rd August, 1974.

Plate 87: Installation of multiple aspect colour light signalling and new track layout at Paddington takes shape in October, 1967 as 'Western' No. D 1048 *Western Lady* takes a Bristol bound train out of the station. Although the road bridge tends to obstruct the work of the cranes, they are to be seen assisting the labour force with the relaying of point work etc.

Plate 88: No. D 1053 *Western Patriarch* is manoeuvred into place on the turntable at Old Oak Common on 15th May, 1976. No. 31 413 and another unidentified Class 31 look on in the background.

'Western' Class 2,700 hp C–C
Diesel Hydraulic Locomotives

D.1000 *Western Enterprise*	D.1017 *Western Warrior*	D.1036 *Western Emperor*	D.1055 *Western Advocate*
D.1001 *Western Pathfinder*	D.1018 *Western Buccaneer*	D.1037 *Western Empress*	D.1056 *Western Sultan*
D.1002 *Western Explorer*	D.1019 *Western Challenger*	D.1038 *Western Sovereign*	D.1057 *Western Chieftain*
D.1003 *Western Pioneer*	D.1020 *Western Hero*	D.1039 *Western King*	D.1058 *Western Nobleman*
D.1004 *Western Crusader*	D.1021 *Western Cavalier*	D.1040 *Western Queen*	D.1059 *Western Empire*
D.1005 *Western Venturer*	D.1022 *Western Sentinel*	D.1041 *Western Prince*	D.1060 *Western Dominion*
D.1006 *Western Stalwart*	D.1023 *Western Fusilier*	D.1042 *Western Princess*	D.1061 *Western Envoy*
D.1007 *Western Talisman*	D.1024 *Western Huntsman*	D.1043 *Western Duke*	D.1062 *Western Courier*
D.1008 *Western Harrier*	D.1025 *Western Guardsman*	D.1044 *Western Duchess*	D.1063 *Western Monitor*
D.1009 *Western Invader*	D.1026 *Western Centurion*	D.1045 *Western Viscount*	D.1064 *Western Regent*
D.1010 *Western Campaigner*	D.1027 *Western Lancer*	D.1046 *Western Marquis*	D.1065 *Western Consort*
D.1011 *Western Thunderer*	D.1028 *Western Hussar*	D.1047 *Western Lord*	D.1066 *Western Prefect*
D.1012 *Western Firebrand*	D.1029 *Western Legionaire*	D.1048 *Western Lady*	D.1067 *Western Druid*
D.1013 *Western Ranger*	D.1030 *Western Musketeer*	D.1049 *Western Monarch*	D.1068 *Western Reliance*
D.1014 *Western Leviathan*	D.1031 *Western Rifleman*	D.1050 *Western Ruler*	D.1069 *Western Vanguard*
D.1015 *Western Champion*	D.1032 *Western Marksman*	D.1051 *Western Ambassador*	D.1070 *Western Gauntlet*
D.1016 *Western Gladiator*	D.1033 *Western Trooper*	D.1052 *Western Viceroy*	D.1071 *Western Renown*
	D.1034 *Western Dragoon*	D.1053 *Western Patriarch*	D.1072 *Western Glory*
	D.1035 *Western Yeoman*	D.1054 *Western Governor*	D.1073 *Western Bulwark*

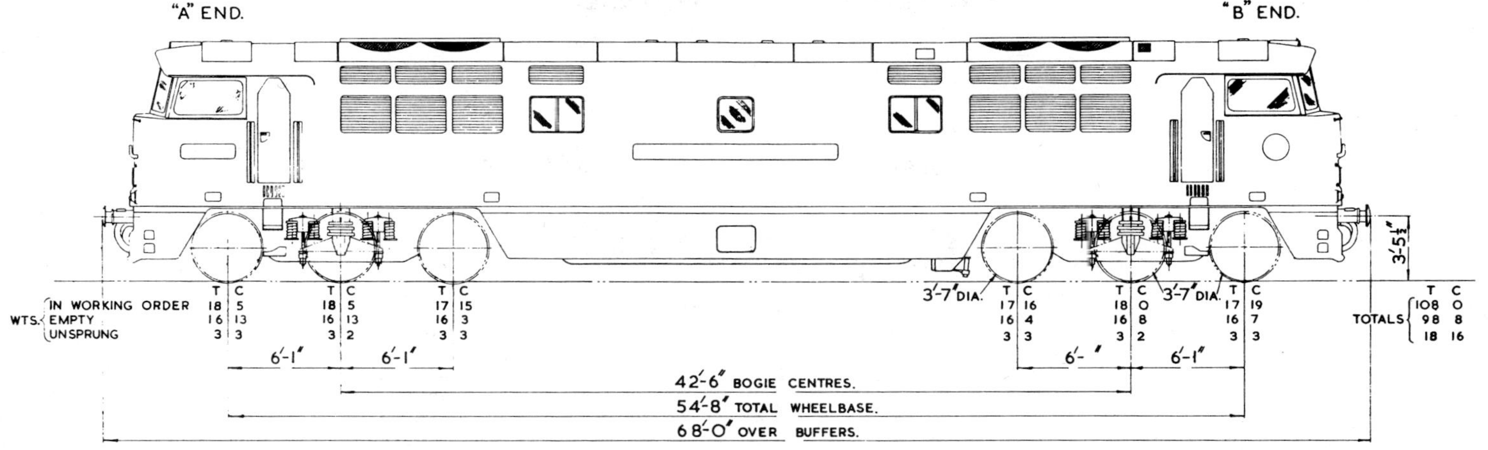

Plate 89: No. D 1031 *Western Rifleman* stands on Bristol Bath Road depot on 31st July, 1970 with the breakdown crane and assorted vehicles including a steam loco tender next to the stop blocks.

Plate 90: Loaded and empty stone trains cross at Merehead Quarry Junction on 20th June, 1975. No. D 1067 *Western Druid* waits to leave with a train of loaded Procors from the Merehead Stone Terminal operated by Foster Yeoman Limited, as No. D 1013 *Western Ranger* (right of the picture) arrives with a train of empties from Westbury.

Plate 91:
Western Class 52, D 1062 *Western Courier* with No. 818 *Glory* standing outside Swindon Works on 24th June, 1976.

Plate 92: 'Western' No. D 1067 *Western Druid* at Truro with 1B81, 08.00 Bristol (Temple Meads) to Penzance on 4th January, 1975. The Falmouth branch diesel multiple unit stands in the bay platform.

Plate 93: The 12.00 Paddington to Swansea service with No. D 1034 *Western Dragoon* standing at Swindon on 25th August, 1971. This station has now been rebuilt with an island platform on the Up side for stopping trains and through lines without platforms primarily for the new High Speed train workings.

Plate 94: Rail enthusiasts visit Kidderminster on 28th March, 1971 for a trip on the Severn Valley Railway. 'Western' No. D 1027 *Western Lancer* stands ready to take the special train back to Plymouth.

Brush Class 47's

Plate 95: Snap! — a line-up at Old Oak Common with three Brush Class 47 locomotives by the turntable on a September morning in 1975. These headcodes apply to South Wales block trains and the picture was specially posed for publicity purposes.

Plate 96; Exit from Paddington — Brush Class 47 No. 47 230 takes the heavily loaded 17.42 commuter service to Oxford out of the station, whilst Class 52 No. D 1005 *Western Venturer* waits for the shunting signal to allow the locomotive to come off Ranelagh Bridge fuelling depot to pick up its train in the station.

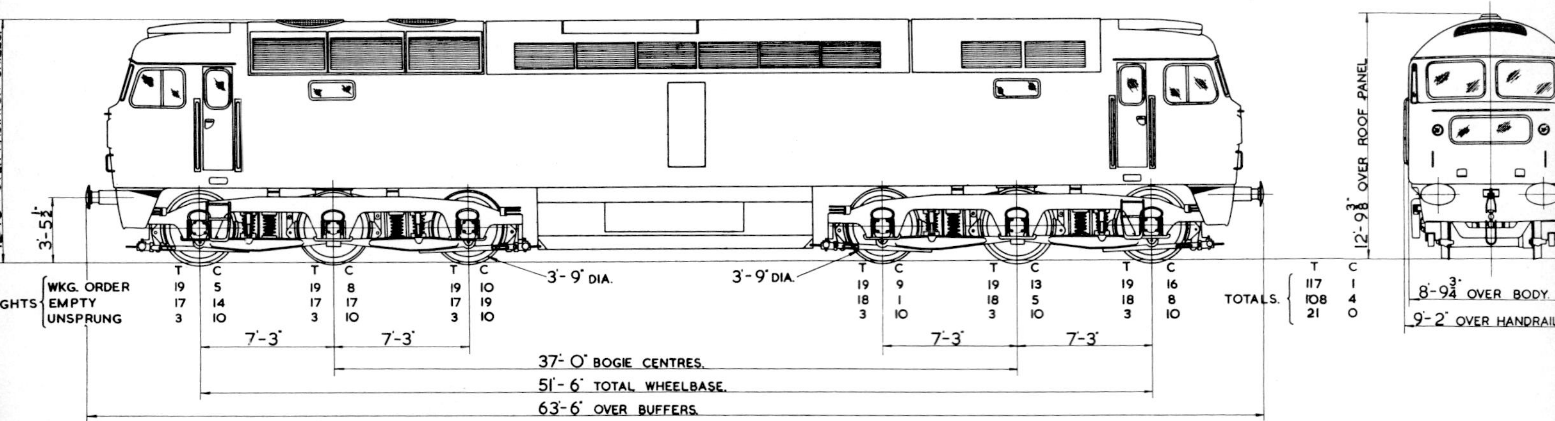

Plate 97: No. 47 426 winds the heavy Sunday 12.20 Aberdeen — Kings Cross express through the rock cutting north of Cove Bay near Aberdeen on 24th March, 1974.

Plate 98: A plume of smoke rises to the heavens as No. 47 064 leaves Hayle and traverses the viaduct with the 10.56 summer Saturdays only service from Paddington to Penzance on 26th July, 1975.

Plate 99: No. 47 547 complete with new front panel marker lights, accelerates away from Grantham Station on 25th September, 1976 with the 11.30 Leeds to Kings Cross Inter-City service.

Plate 100: A train of oil tank wagons hauled by No. 47 331 heads north on the Midland main line alongside the M1 Motorway near Mill Hill in pouring rain on 2nd October, 1974.

Plate 101: No. 47 137 crosses the River Avon at Fladbury, between Evesham and Pershore on the single line from Moreton-in-Marsh to Norton Junction with the 10.05 Paddington to Worcester (Shrub Hill) on 14th June, 1975. The other section of the line that has been singled on the Oxford — Worcester route is between Wolvercote Junction and Ascott-under-Wychwood.

Plate 102: Liverpool (Lime Street) Station on Sunday, 8th December, 1974, with No. 47 195 (formerly 1845) awaiting departure from the station with 1V83 10.40 Liverpool to Plymouth train.

Plate 103: Brush Class 47 No. 1801, since renumbered 47 320, stands at Old Oak Common with a train of cement wagons on 30th July, 1971.

Brush class 47 2600-2750 bhp
Co - Co

47 076 (1660) *City of Truro*	47 080 (1665) *Titan*	47 088 (1674) *Samson*
47 077 (1661) *North Star*	47 081 (1666) *Odin*	47 089 (1675) *Amazon*
47 078 (1663) *Sir Daniel Gooch*	47 082 (1667) *Atlas*	47 090 (1676) *Vulcan*
47 079 (1664) *George Jackson Churchward*	47 083 (1668) *Orion*	47 091 (1677) *Thor*
	47 085 (1670) *Mammoth*	47 484 (1662) *Isambard Kingdom Brunel*
	47 086 (1672) *Colossus*	47 538 (1669) *Python*
	47 087 (1673) *Cyclops*	

Plate 104: No. 47 086 *Colossus* at the head of the 09.30 Paddington to Penzance service approaching the end of the line on 7th July, 1976, over half an hour late as a reaction of the preceding 08.30 Paddington to Plymouth train having a locomotive failure at Reading. A Class 45 locomotive and coaching stock await their next duties. The building on the main road in the background is the Heliport for the Penzance — Isles of Scilly service.

Plate 105: Stratford No. 47 155 was removed from its bogies and taken by road to West Thurrock Power Station in February, 1976 to act as a stationary exciter for the 300 mw turbo-alternator. The normal exciter required repairs estimated to take four months and the locomotive's output provided an identical source of power.

Plate 106: A picturesque scene in Harbury cutting between Leamington and Banbury on Sunday 27th April, 1975 with a special train of air-braked MGR hoppers from the Midlands bound for Didcot power station, with No. 47 321 doing the heavy work!

Plate 107: The up 'Aberdonian' 10.45 Aberdeen to Kings Cross headed by Brush Class 47 No. 1975 passes under the spectacular semaphore signal gantry at Ferryhill, Aberdeen on 21st March, 1974.

Plate 108: No. 47 136 storms out of Oxford station with the 14.05 Paddington to Birmingham (New Street) on 16th October, 1976. Part of the fuelling facilities with flood-lighting can be seen in the bottom right hand corner of the photograph.

Plate 109: A train of hopper wagons from the Western Region rounds the bend on the up line under Battledown Flyover at Worting Junction near Basingstoke on 27th April, 1974 with No.47 137 in charge.

Plate 110: No. 47 076 *City of Truro* brings an inter regional block train of Blue Circle cement wagons through Denmark Hill station, over the electrified SR lines in South East London on 18th February, 1976.

Plate 111: Engineering work necessitated AL7 Bo-Bo electric Class 87 No. 87 018 having its pantograph lowered and submitting to diesel haulage by Brush Class 47 No. 47 491, seen near Great Bridgeford, north of Stafford on 4th May, 1975.

Plate 112: Amidst interested spectators No. 47 185 is about to depart from Radstock for Westbury on 2nd March, 1974 after collecting newly repaired B P Chemicals Procor wagon PR 8234 with brake van.

Plate 113: No. 47 542 negotiates the pointwork approaching Darlington with the 14.35 Newcastle to Kings Cross via York, Leeds and Wakefield on 22nd April, 1976.

Plate 114: The railways work round the clock as this picture proves. No. D 1664 *George Jackson Churchward* pulls away from Milford Haven oil storage depot with a Gulf oil train.

Plate 115: A block train of fuel-oil wagons passes through a non-platform road at Worcester (Shrub Hill) on 31st July, 1970 behind a rather dirty No. 1912, now renumbered 47 235, on its way from Waterston to Albion.

Plate 116: Open day for the visitors at Crewe works on 20th September, 1975. Brush Class 47 No. 47 046 (formerly 1628) is seen in the process of conversion and renumbering to 47 601. This locomotive was fitted with the same type of engine used in the Class 56s and was converted for test evaluation purposes prior to the ordering of the new class.

47's at rest

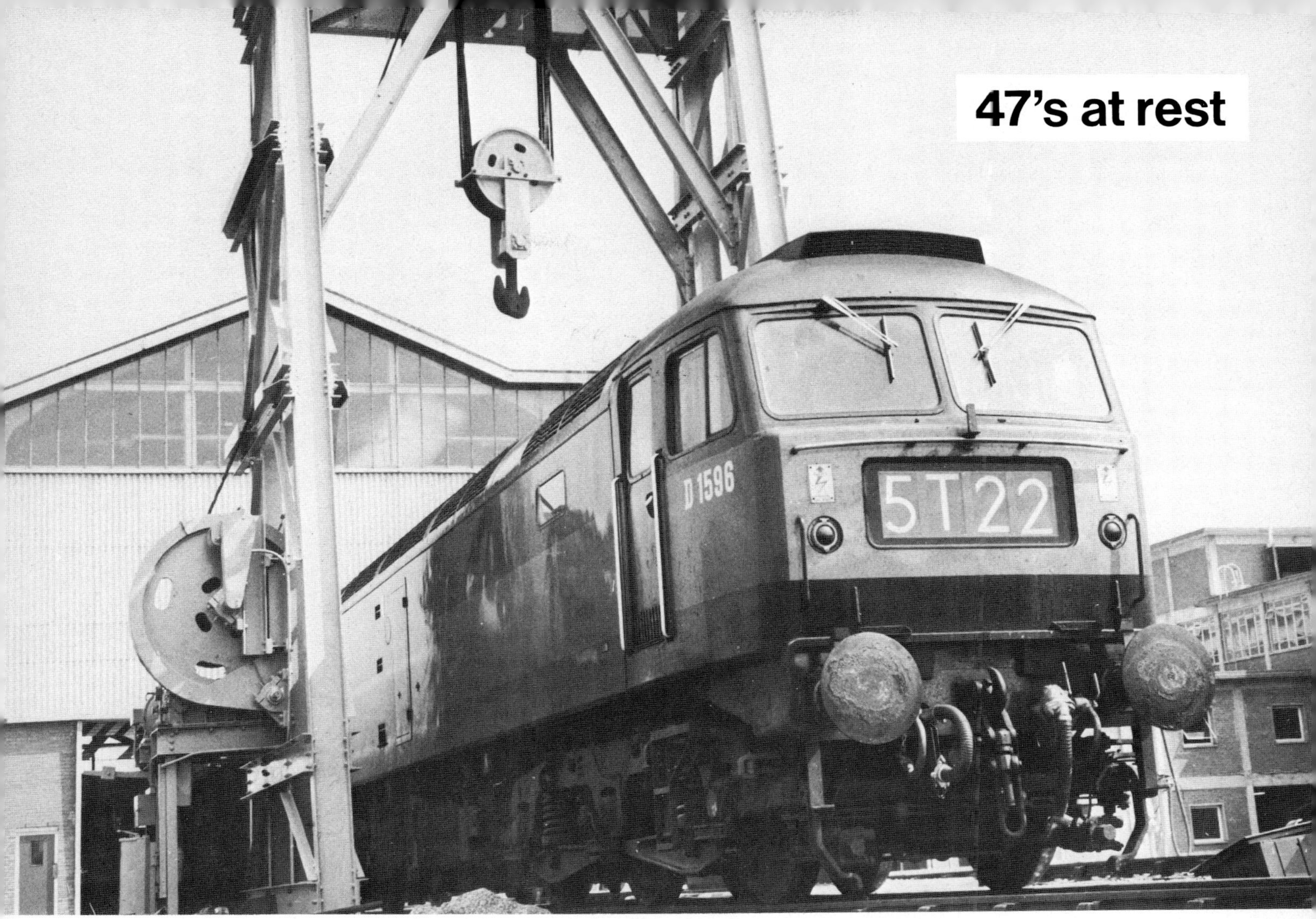

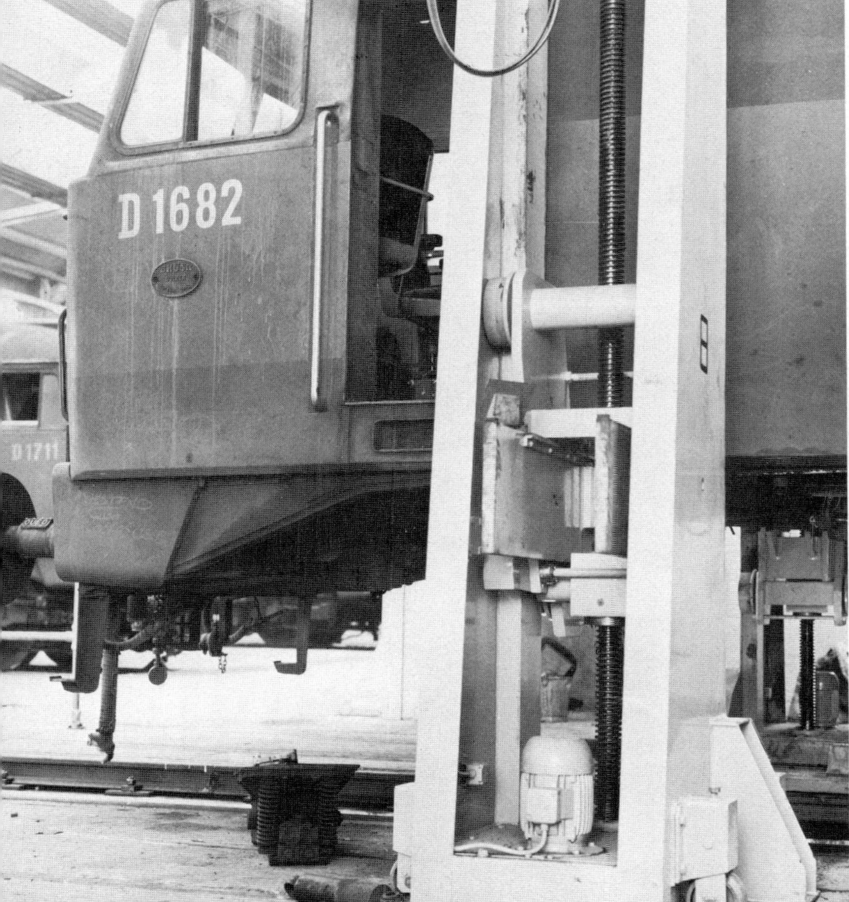

Plate 117: Cardiff Canton depot with No. D 1596 (since renumbered 47 470) under the 40 ton electric hoist in September, 1974.

Plate 118: Can I have my wheels back? One of the synchronised jacks helping to keep No. D 1682 suspended during bogie changing operations. No D 1711 looks on to the left of the picture.

Plate 119: Close up of the front end of No. 1606, now renumbered 47 029, at Landore diesel depot on 17th May, 1970.

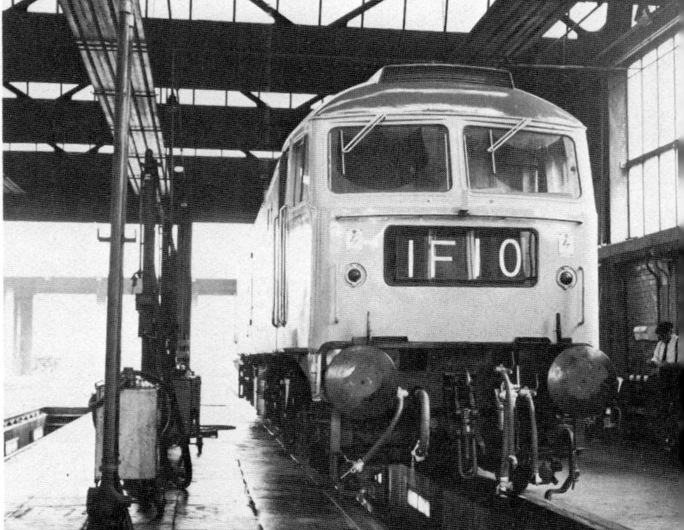

Over Shap

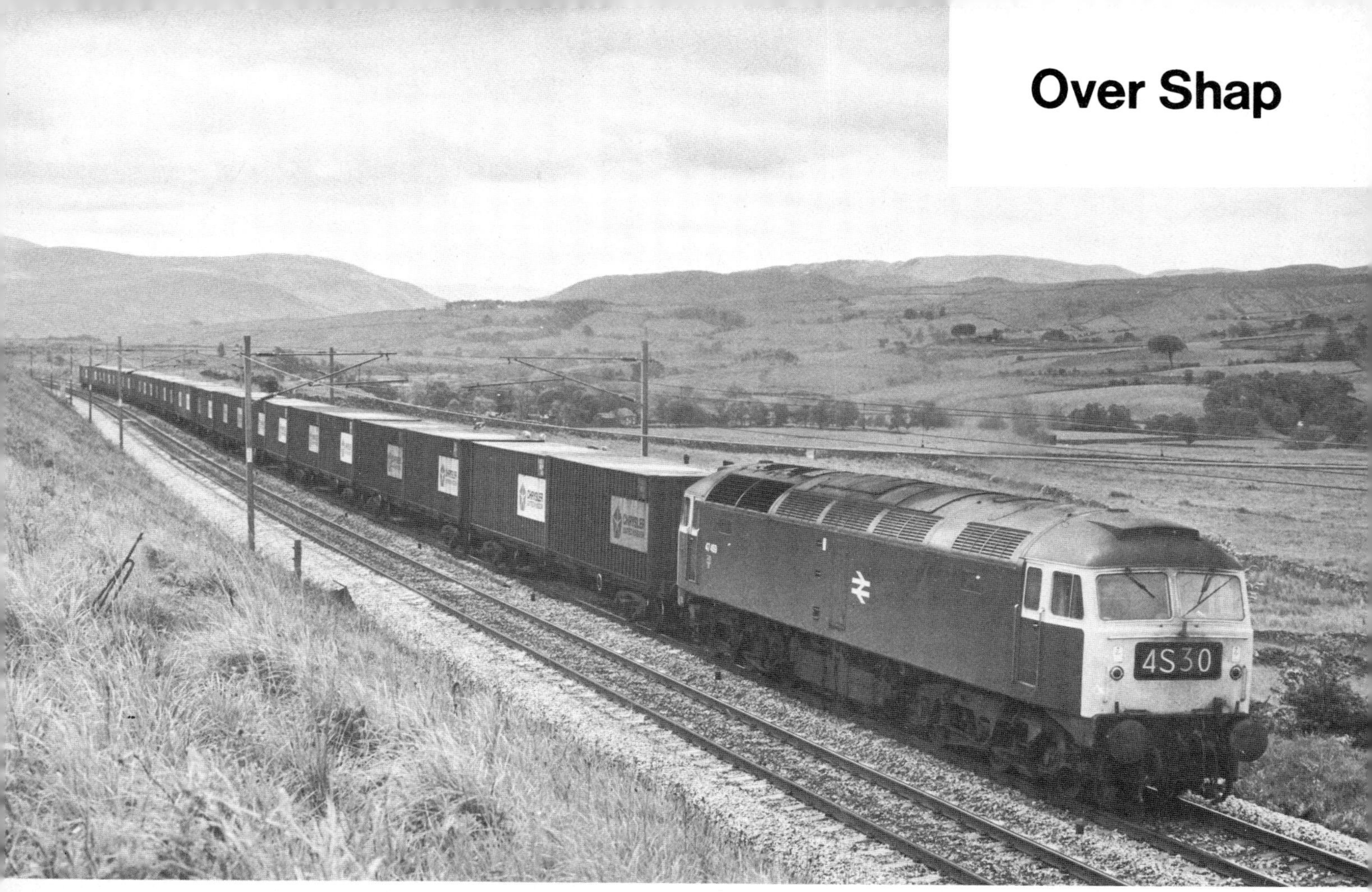

Plate 120: No. 47 469 climbs Shap Fell on 12th June, 1974 with a Chrysler (UK) block train bound for Linwood.

Plate 121: Type 2 Class 25 No. 25 042 drifts down Shap Fell with an engineers' Permanent Way train on 12th June, 1974.

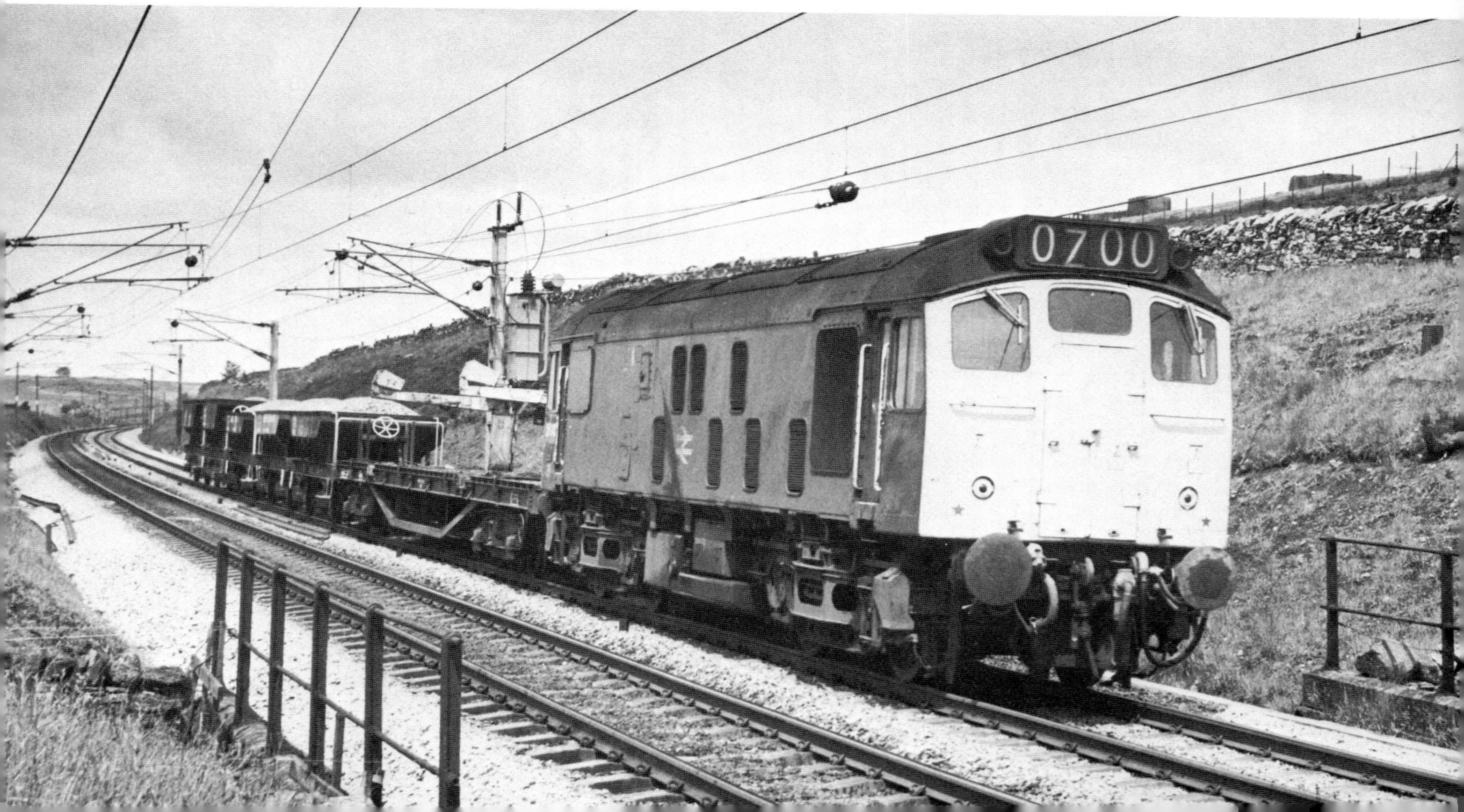

Plate 122: English Electric type 4 Co-Co diesel Class 50 No. 50 042 passes near the former Shap station on 2nd April, 1974 with an up Anglo-Scottish express. A total of fifty Class 50 locomotives were built and were first introduced in 1967 prior to the full electrification of the West Coast main line route through to Glasgow. All these locomotives have now been transferred for use on Western Region.

Plate 123: Another Class 50 photographed near Shap station on 2nd April, 1974, this time No. 50 022 with the 11.58 Carlisle to Euston passenger service.

Freight Transfer Locomotives

Plate 124: The first of the Class 20s — No. D 8000 poses for the camera prior to taking up freight duties.

Plate 125: North British Bo-Bo type 1 diesel electric locomotive No. D 8400 awaits its next turn of duty at Temple Mills Hump yard, East London in May, 1959. These locomotives were first introduced in 1958 and the entire class has now been withdrawn from traffic.

Plate 126: English Electric Bo-Bo Class 20 No. D 8039 hauls a cross-London mixed freight transfer service over the electrified lines at Kensal Green Junction in 1959.

at Paddington~Class 50's...

Plate 127: A change of scene from Shap — a recently transferred English Electric type 4 Co-Co Class 50 heads out of Paddington on an Inter-City departure, the afternoon sunlight glistening against the profile of the locomotive and the roadbridges above.

Plate 128: The Class 50s dominate at Ranelagh Bridge, Paddington on 21st May, 1975. No's. 50 049 and 50 046 are standing awaiting their next turn of duty whilst the secondman guides his driver back onto the depot with 50 049.

...and elsewhere

Plate 129: 21st October, 1973 was a wet morning at Liverpool (Lime Street). Class 50 No. 438, since renumbered 50 038, stands with the 11.40 for Plymouth waiting for departure.

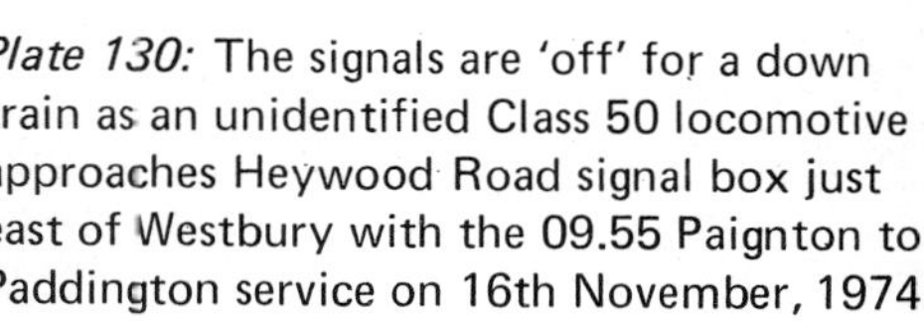

Plate 130: The signals are 'off' for a down train as an unidentified Class 50 locomotive approaches Heywood Road signal box just east of Westbury with the 09.55 Paignton to Paddington service on 16th November, 1974.

Plate 131: No. 50 033 arrives at Bristol (Temple Meads) with the air conditioned passenger coaching stock and Mark 1 BG leading, for the 15.45 Sunday service to Paddington on 19th October, 1975.

Plate 132: Amidst a setting of leafy trees the 12.50 Penzance to Crewe perishables train leaves St Erth on 30th July, 1975 behind No. 50 019.

Plate 133: No. 50 048 heads out of Reading on the down main line past the 100 mph sign with the 16.15 Paddington — Weston-super-Mare service on 7th April, 1976. Now that the High Speed trains are in operation on this line there is an 80 mph maximum speed restriction through Reading going up to 125 mph west of the station.

Not a pretty sight!

Plate 134: Class 37 No. 6906 pauses at Gloucester whilst making its way to Doncaster works for repair on 30th December, 1973. The locomotive had been involved in a mishap at Margam when the freight vehicles had run away in the hump yard causing extensive damage to the rear cab and very regrettably killing the guard.

Plate 135: Can we have our engine back? An error in shunting operations near Marine Colliery, Cwm on 29th January, 1975 led to the derailment and toppling to the foot of an embankment of Class 37 No. 37 143 and the leading vehicles of a 32 wagon train. The wagons were removed, but the 105 ton locomotive remained on its side until 4th August when it was successfully removed. (Earlier attempts in March had proved abortive). This picture shows the locomotive in a sorry state on 10th May, 1975.

Plate 136: No. 37 119 stands in Doncaster works yard awaiting repair after a collision in the north east.

Plate 137: A very battered English Electric Class 40 No. 40 189 stands in Crewe works yard awaiting attention on 20th December, 1975.

Plate 138: A fine picture of No. 55 014 *The Duke of Wellington's Regiment* leaving Newcastle. The telephoto lens produces a rather interesting foreshortening of the massive engine.

55 001	(9001)	*St. Paddy*
55 002	(9002)	*The King's Own Yorkshire Light Infantry*
55 003	(9003)	*Meld*
55 004	(9004)	*Queen's Own Highlander*
55 005	(9005)	*The Prince of Wales's Own Regiment of York*
55 006	(9006)	*The Fife & Forfar Yeomanry*
55 007	(9007)	*Pinza*
55 008	(9008)	*The Green Howards*
55 009	(9009)	*Alycidon*
55 010	(9010)	*The King's Own Scottish Borderer*
55 011	(9011)	*The Royal Northumberland Fusiliers*
55 012	(9012)	*Crepello*
55 013	(9013)	*The Black Watch*
55 014	(9014)	*The Duke of Wellington's Regiment*
55 015	(9015)	*Tulyar*
55 016	(9016)	*Gordon Highlander*
55 017	(9017)	*The Durham Light Infantry*
55 018	(9018)	*Ballymoss*
55 019	(9019)	*Royal Highland Fusilier*
55 020	(9020)	*Nimbus*
55 021	(9021)	*Argyll & Sutherland Highlander*
55 022	(9000)	*Royal Scots Grey*

Plate 139: Deltic diesel electric Class 55 No. D 9012 *Crepello* leaves Leeds with 'The West Riding' in the 1960s. Rather pleasant to recall the maroon coaches and semaphore signals once more.

Plate 140: Class 55 No. 55 016 *Gordon Highlander* pulls out of Peterborough on 27th August, 1974, with 1S35 the 14.00 Kings Cross to Aberdeen air conditioned Inter-City service. Several of the smaller and less powerful Class 31s and 47s can be seen in the vicinity.

Plate 141: No it's not a steam engine! It's Deltic No. 55 005 *The Prince of Wales's Own Regiment of Yorkshire* setting back into one of the platforms at Kings Cross on 23rd July, 1975 to pick up its train and make ready for a departure. A Brush Class 47 stands on shed on the right of the picture.

Plate 142: Kings Cross in all its glory on 12th June, 1975 with Deltic No. 55 018 *Ballymoss* winding its way out of the station with the 11.25 Inter-City service to Leeds, complete with air conditioned coaching stock. A Class 47 waits with its train at the adjoining platform next to a Class 31 coupling up to a set of empty coaching stock for Finsbury Park.

Plate 143: The overall roof at York station is not dissimilar to that of Kings Cross and provides the setting for the 14.00 Kings Cross to Aberdeen service on 13th July, 1971 with Class 55 No. 9012 *Crepello* at the head of the train.

Plate 144: An unusual visitor under the wires at Stratford is No. 55 013 *The Black Watch* about to pass through the station on 2nd March, 1976.

Plate 145: Deltic No. 55 011 *The Royal Northumberland Fusiliers* wends its way out of Doncaster station and accelerates away on the main line with the 14.10 Newcastle to Kings Cross train on 7th May, 1974.

Plate 146: A night close-up of the nameboard and emblem on Deltic No. 9000 *Royal Scots Grey* standing on the 20.30 Kings Cross to Edinburgh overnight service, 10th November, 1971.

Plate 147: An aerial view of busy Newcastle with its complex track layout which includes several diamond crossings. Class 45 No. 45 023 *The Royal Pioneer Corps* pulls out of the station with the empty coaching stock from the 07.40 from Cardiff whilst an unidentified Deltic runs alongside with the down 'Flying Scotsman' on 3rd November, 1976.

Plate 148: A side close up view of No. 55 003 *Meld* about to leave Kings Cross with the 15.15 Inter-City service to Leeds on 28th April, 1974.

Plate 149: Have we got all the carriages? — the driver leans out of the cab and looks back as Class 55 No. 9020 *Nimbus* accelerates out of York with the 11.00 Edinburgh to Kings Cross Inter-City passenger service on 18th July, 1972.

Plate 150: Deltic No. 9015 *Tulyar* (subsequently renumbered 55 015) heads the 'Flying Scotsman' through Peterborough with the North signal box and a Class 47 locomotive in green livery behind, on 14th June, 1969.

The Blue Pullmans

Plate 151: The Metropolitan Cammell Pullman units were built in 1959 and entered passenger service the following year. Five trains were introduced, two of which were of six cars for first class passengers only and three of eight cars with both first and second class accommodation. The six car sets were for the St Pancras — Manchester service and the eight car trains for Paddington — Wolverhampton and Bristol. The 'Blue Pullmans' as they are called, were subsequently used exclusively on Western Region's London —South Wales/Bristol and Birmingham services, although the latter was discontinued from 3rd March, 1967.

In the early 1960's the Birmingham Pullman is seen at Paddington attracting much interest from passengers and staff.

Plate 152: An eight car Pullman set shining in all its glory speeds towards the capital under a clear lower quadrant semaphore signal.

Plate 153: The scene at Paddington on 12th September, 1960 with the immaculately turned out 'Blue Pullman' units side by side waiting to depart for Birmingham (on the left) and Bristol (on the right). The drivers and secondmen were suitably attired in white coats and caps with blue piping.

Plate 154: The 'Blue Pullmans' underwent a change of livery to silver-grey with dark blue stripe along the window line. This picture shows the 09.00 Paddington to Swansea train at Newport station on 31st October, 1967, in its final condition before withdrawal.

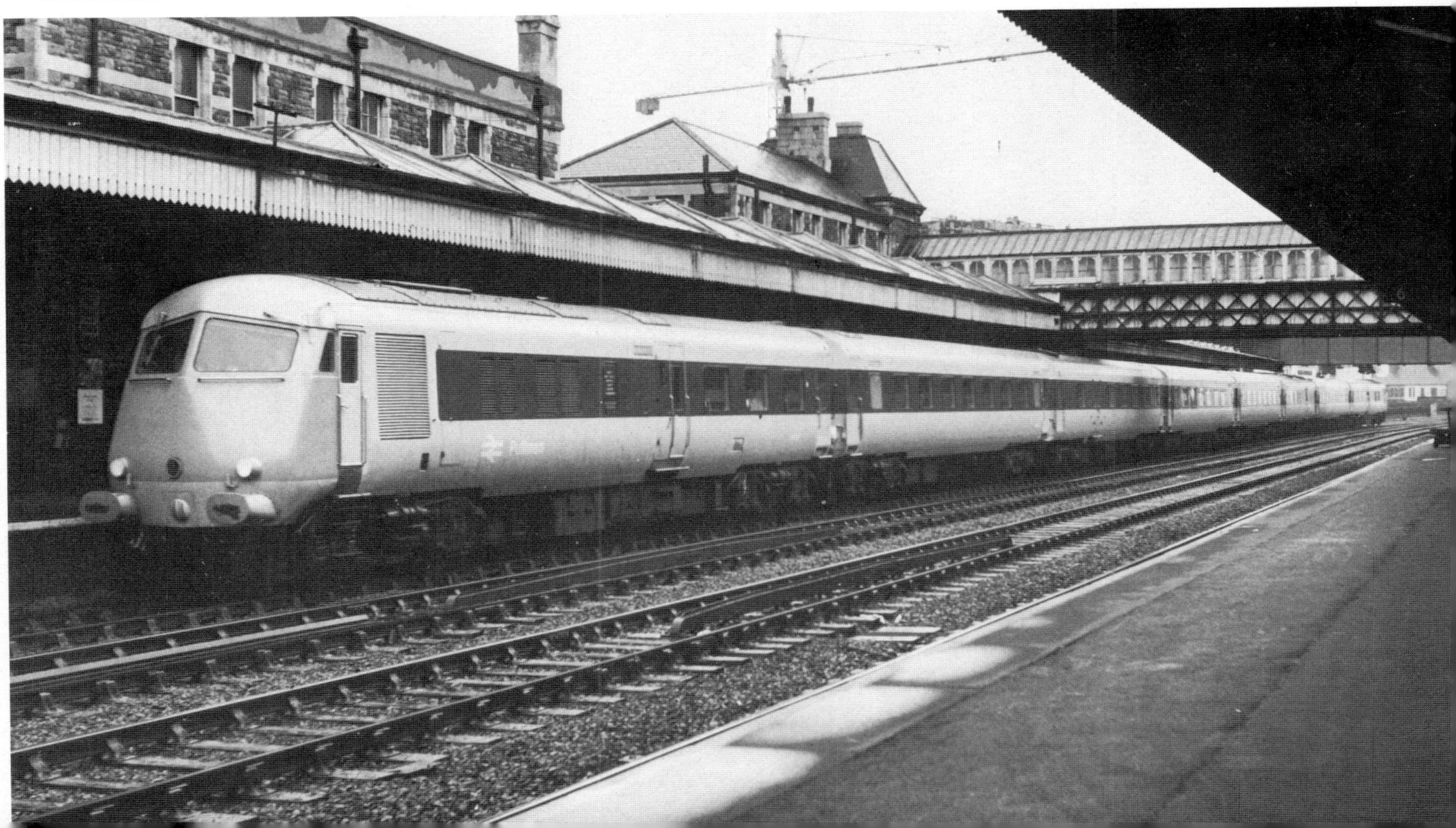

Class 33's

Plate 155: Birmingham Railway Carriage & Wagon Co. type 3 Bo-Bo Class 33 No. 33 206 pauses between duties at Stewarts Lane depot, South London on 30th June, 1974.

Plate 156: The trees have a bare wintry look on a cold mid-January day in 1976, as No. 33 063 heads a train of tank wagons between Mottingham and Lee on its way from Northfleet to the London Midland Region via Kew.

Plate 157: Class 33 No. 6582 heads up the Brighton main line towards Clapham Junction with a ballast train as a down 4-sub electric multiple unit enters the cutting with a South Western Division service from Waterloo.

Plate 158: There is plenty of activity at Weymouth Quay after the Channel Islands boat has arrived on 1st July, 1974. No. 33 107 complete with flashing light and warning bell on the front, couples up to the coaches forming the 15.50 train to Waterloo whilst more passengers arrive by taxi and on foot.

Plate 159: An up parcels service from Margate to Bricklayers Arms on 12th May, 1973 ambles along between Hildenborough and Sevenoaks with Class 33 No. 6596 in charge (note miniature snow ploughs).

Plate 160: No. 33 205 makes light work of a Blue Circle Cement block train heading along the Dartford Loop line between Mottingham and New Eltham in South East London on 20th May, 1975.

Plate 161: Class 33 locomotive No. D6536 storms away from Bournemouth with a Weymouth bound 4 - TC set in original all-blue livery. The picture was taken in June, 1967 just before the implementation of full diesel services.

Plate 162: The 06.45 Yeovil to Waterloo passenger service headed by Class 33 No. 6524 approaches Clapham Junction on 15th August, 1972.

Under the Wires

Plate 163: Class 37 No. 37 034 pulls slowly through Colchester station towards London with a Norwich to Liverpool Street service on 12th May, 1974.

Plate 164: Leaving Liverpool (Lime Street) station with the 10.10 train to Newcastle on 23rd September, 1976 is a rather dirty Class 46 locomotive No. 46 038 (formerly No. 175).

Plate 165: An unidentified Class 40 locomotive heads a train of maroon coaching stock through Liverpool (Lime Street) cutting amidst the grime of the bygone age of steam. Despite electrification many diesel locomotives still work through the approach tunnels to the station. This picture was taken 'under the wires' in June, 1962.

Plate 166: Class 40 No. D 202 speeds through Bethnal Green station on 6th August, 1958 with a mixed rake of stock, including at least two ex LNER Gresley vehicles, forming the 15.45 Norwich (Thorpe) to Liverpool Street service. The then non-electrified Enfield and Chingford line platforms are on the left.

Plate 167: Class 25 No. 7530 climbs Camden Bank on its way out of Euston with a down parcels service on 16th May, 1973. An all-stations d.c. electric train on the local Watford to Euston line can be seen to the left of the photograph.

Plate 168: A train of empty stock from Stratford carriage sidings makes its way up Brentwood bank to Harwick Parkeston Quay for a boat train working on 26th April, 1973, behind Class 37 No. 6712.

Class 27's

Plate 169: A train of coal empties and covered wagons hauled by Class 27 No 5347 in green livery, passes near Kittybrewster on the approach to Aberdeen on 27th March, 1974.

Plate 170: Class 27 No. 27 012 passes under clear signals, through Dundee Tay Bridge station on a 'Rangers Football Supporters Club' special charter train from Glasgow to Aberdeen on 7th December, 1974.

Plate 171: The 10.28 Perth to Manchester vans train trundles between Kinbuck and Dunblane on 24th May, 1976, motive power being provided by No. 27 044.

Class 44's

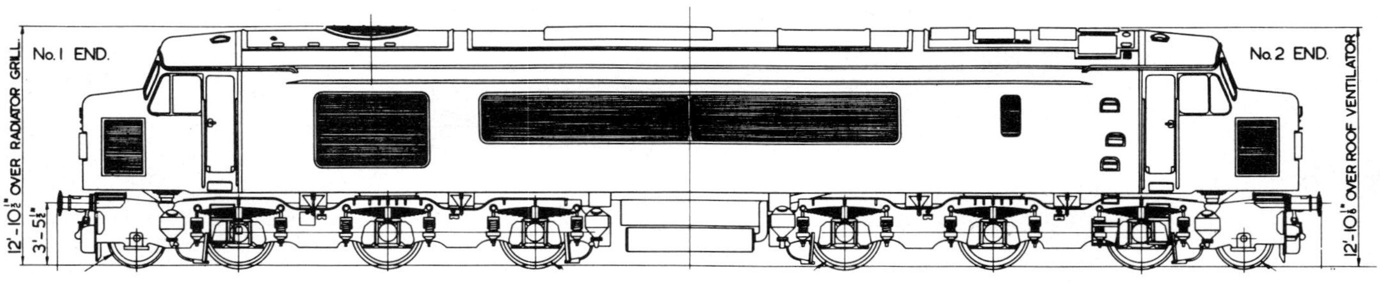

Plate 172: 'Peak' Class 44 No. D 5 *Cross Fell,* since renumbered 44 005, approaches Weaver Junction on a Euston to Liverpool train in April, 1961. The train consists of all maroon coaching stock with side destination boards throughout.

Peak class 44, 2300 bhp
1 Co Co 1

44 001 (1) *Scafell Pike*	44 003 (3) *Skiddaw*	44 007 (7) *Ingleborough*
44 002 (2) *Helvellyn*	44 004 (4) *Great Gable*	44 008 (8) *Penyghent*
	44 005 (5) *Cross Fell*	44 009 (9) *Snowdon*
	44 006 (6) *Whernside*	44 010 (10) *Tryfan*

Plate 173: Stafford station was undergoing renovation and reconstruction in 1962, as the temporary corrugated bridge work indicates. 'Peak' Class 44 No. D 4 *Great Gable* calls with a down express.

Plate 174: The same locomotive as above, this time renumbered 44 004, heads a line of four 'Peak' Class 44s outside Toton depot on 31st August, 1975. On parade with No. 44 004 are No's 44 006 *Whernside,* 44 009 *Snowdon,* and 44 005 *Cross Fell* (see plate 172). On the side lines are Class 20 No. 20 140 and another unidentified locomotive of the same Class.

Men at Work

Plate 175: Driver portrait with a close up of Class 31
No. 31 299.

Plate 176: A driver's turn of duty commences as he
joins his locomotive, in this case Class 47 No. D1613.

Plate 177: Inside the cab of the same
locomotive as plate 176 Class 47 No. D1613
— this time speeding through Slough with
the speedometer recording 95 mph.

Class 40's

Plate 178: Class 40 No. 40 076 with a Locomotive Club of Great Britain special charter train returning from Ulverston to Carnforth along the attractive coastal stretch near Grange-over-Sands. This tour incorporated steam traction on the Leeds to Carnforth route with locomotive No. 92220 *Evening Star.*

Plate 179: 14.05 Perth to Aberdeen parcels train headed by Class 40 No. 280 passes a diesel multiple unit local passenger working just outside Perth on 14th November, 1973.

Plate 180: Class 40 No. 349 brings an up express towards Kings Cross on 22nd March, 1973. It is about to enter Copenhagen tunnel which is situated on the London side of Finsbury Park.

Plate 181: A local goods train conveying loaded pipe wagons trundles past Polmadie depot near Glasgow on 7th September, 1974, behind Class 40 No. 210.

Plate 182: An up West Coast Express headed by Class 40 No. D231 *Sylvania* passes a disused semaphore junction signal near Carlisle Kingmoor in March, 1963.

Plate 183: No. 40 120 gives a tow to sister locomotive No. 40 141 at Guide Bridge, Manchester on 21st August, 1974 — it seems likely that No. 40 141 has failed and is being taken back to the depot for repairs.

Plate 184: Night departure — Class 40 No. 257 is about to leave March with an air braked car-carrying train in October, 1973. This picture was taken with a time exposure on the camera — unfortunately the semaphore signals behind the train came off during the operation with a rather confusing result!

Plate 185: Chinley station is now but a shadow of its former self as can be seen from this view taken on 21st September, 1976. The 07.28 Harwich, Parkeston Quay to Manchester service leaves the station with No. 40 054 in charge.

Plate 186: No. 40 107 stands at Workington on 19th April, 1975 with a set of empty stock. Scotches can be seen under the front wheels of the locomotive as a safety precaution to ensure that the train does not roll forward.

Plate 187: Crewe Works Open Day on 20th September, 1975 — an immaculate No. 40 103 stands ready for the cameras.

D.M.U's-The mainstay of Local travel

Plate 188: The brilliant sun light penetrates the roof of Reading motive power depot on 7th April, 1976. Western Region now has a system of numbering d.m.u. sets with the prefix letter indicating the broad area to which they are allocated, i.e. L : London; P : Plymouth; C : Cardiff; B : Bristol. The unit furthest from the camera is a three car suburban set, with Pressed Steel Company motor brake second, Class 117/2 car No. W51335 visible. The unit on the near side line is a Gloucester Railway Carriage & Wagon Company set with Class 119/1 car No. W 51078 in the picture, originally this was Plymouth based and was probably reallocated to Reading as a result of the reorganisation which released all the Swindon built Inter-City sets from the London area.

Plate 189: Swindon built three car cross-country units in original livery, stand in Cardiff Canton motive power depot on 24th February, 1962. The newly provided d.m.u. inspection roads provide easy access to the underfloor equipment on these trains.

Plate 190: A Shrewsbury bound train on the Central Wales line approaches the Sugar Loaf Mountain which is about seven miles north east of Llandovery and dominates a long and picturesque valley. The train is a Swindon cross-country set with the trailer car missing. An interesting feature is that locomotives and d.m.u.'s working this line are specially fitted with headlights, mainly because of the many ungated crossings on the route.

Plate 191: A Metropolitan-Cammell 3 car d.m.u. heads away from Harrogate on 22nd May, 1959, with a local service for Bradford Exchange.

Plate 192: A 4 car Birmingham Railway Carriage & Wagon Co. d.m.u. leaves York on 21st May, 1959 with a Harrogate service.

Single Car Unit

Plate 193: Gloucester Railway Carriage & Wagon Company Class 128 motor parcels van No. M 55988 forms a local parcels service approaching Manchester (Piccadilly) on 22nd September, 1976. These cars were introduced in 1958, with two BUT (Leyland Albion) 230 bhp engines, giving adequate power to haul several parcel vans when the need arises.

Plate 194: Twyford bay platform on 29th July, 1972 with the 16.50 (Sundays) service to Henley-on-Thames awaiting connecting passengers from the d.m.u. train from London just arrived on the down relief line. The single power car is a Pressed Steel Company Class 121 motor brake second No. W 55031, one of sixteen, all of which are allocated to the Western Region for branch and local services.

Plate 195: Gloucester Railway Carriage & Wagon Company Class 122 Motor brake second single power car forming the 12.20 Stratford upon Avon to Leamington Spa service approaches Hatton West Junction on 19th October, 1974. The guard seems to be taking the fresh air, whilst tree clipping is in progress by the junction signal.

Plate 196: A Pressed Steel Company Class 121 Motor brake second single power car operates the service between Maiden Newton and Bridport on 12th April, 1975, seen departing from Toller station. Sad to relate, this line closed on 5th May, 1975 after well over a century of service to the community. Toller station was originally opened on 31st March, 1862 and rebuilt in 1905; it was reduced to an unstaffed halt in April, 1966.

The Trans-Pennine Sets

Plate 197: A Swindon built five-car Class 124/1 Trans-Pennine set with motor composite vehicle No. E 51967 leading, stands at Selby station on 14th June, 1974 forming the 09.10 Liverpool to Hull service. Introduced in 1960, these units brought new standards of comfort to cross country services over the Pennines.

Plate 198: Leaving Leeds City station with the 15.45 Hull to Liverpool train on 20th September, 1975 is a Class 124/1 Trans-Pennine unit with motor composite vehicle No. E 51956 leading. The standard BR blue and grey livery seems to suit them rather better than the original green.

Plate 199: Trans-Pennine Class 124/1 motor composite vehicle No. E 51958 leading a five-car set working the 11.10 Liverpool — Hull train on 22nd September, 1976, wends its way out of Manchester Victoria station. The headcode display panel is out of use as a result of current BR policy.

More D.M.U's

Plate 200: Windermere station has lost much of its former glory and the lifted track and disused platform tell their own tale. It is now only used by diesel multiple units from Oxenholme and on 22nd May, 1976 the 16.55 departure was formed of a British Rail Derby works built Class 108/2 two car set comprising Driving Trailer Composite (leading) No. M 56248 and Motor Brake Second No. M 50965.

Plate 201: A two car Cravens Unit (car No's. E 51277 and E 56439) forming the 17.23 service to Peterborough leaves Norwich (Thorpe) station platform 4 on 25th June, 1975. A Metropolitan Cammell three car set and a rake of coaching stock wait in the sidings for their next turn of duty. To assist operating staff, units based on Norwich have the maintenance day and date and set number shown at the top of the offside cab windscreen.

Plate 202: Manchester (Victoria) station on 22nd September, 1976. The 13.30 to Llandudno is formed of a refurbished three car Metropolitan Cammell set, Class 144 car No. M 56348 complete with tail lamp at the rear. Just across the way is the 13.45 train to Blackpool (North) with Birmingham Railway Carriage & Wagon Company Class 104/1 motor composite car No. M 50523 featuring in the picture.

Plate 203: The 15.15 Hereford to Birmingham (New Street) service leaves Hereford on 5th October, 1974, formed of a British Rail Swindon built cross country unit in Inter-City livery, with Class 120/2 car No. W 50693 leading the way. Hereford now figures predominantly in the 'Return to Steam' tours programme with three of the steam locomotives used on these special trains being housed at the Bulmers Steam Depot, a mile or so from the main station.

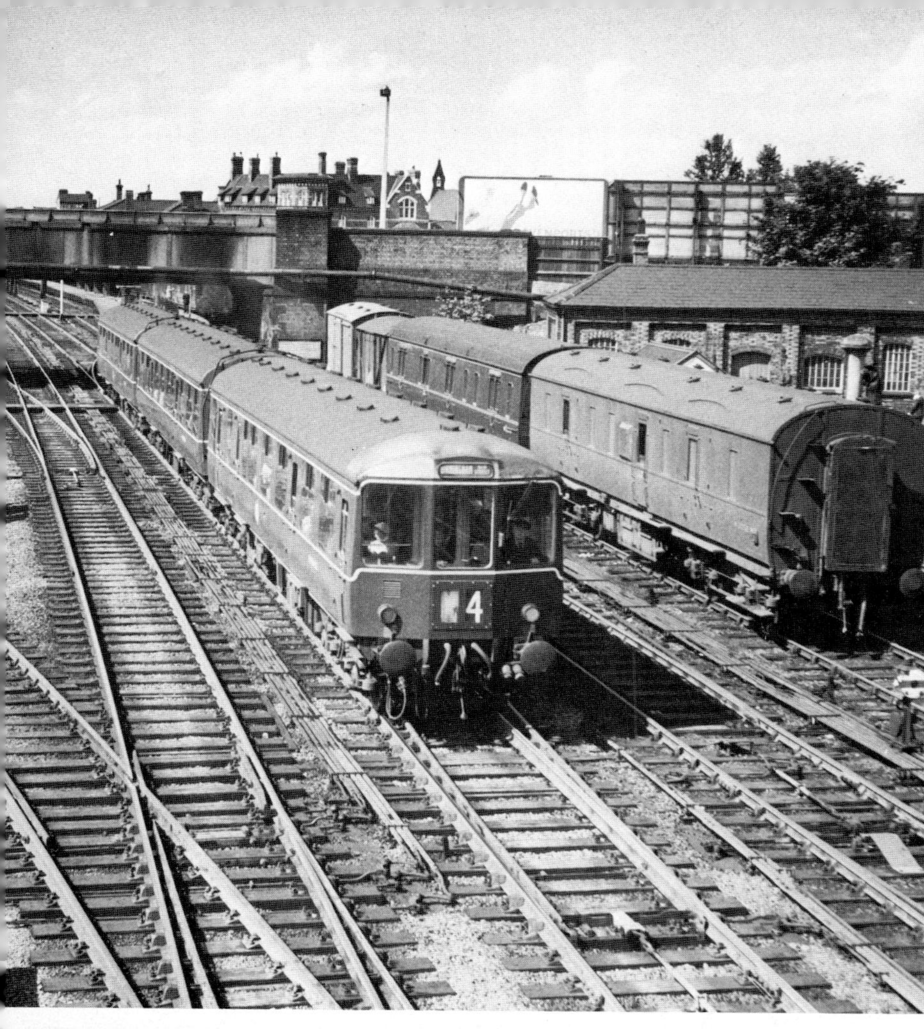

Plate 204: A Birmingham Railway Carriage & Wagon three car unit for Birmingham (New Street) leaves Stafford on 11th August, 1958.

Plate 205: A Swindon built three car cross-country set, with Class 120/2 motor second car No. SC 51790 at the front, forms the 13.43 Aberdeen to Inverness service on 27th March, 1974, accelerating away from the outskirts of Aberdeen near Kittybrewster.

Plate 206: Dwarfed by the picturesque Highland hills, a Metropolitan Cammell three car d.m.u. climbs out of Crianlarich on a Glasgow to Oban service in June, 1974.

Plate 207: Two three car Pressed Steel Company suburban d.m.u. sets formed a special train over the closed Newbury — Welford Park branch where delighted enthusiasts had time to wander over the track and take photographs. The closed signal box can be seen on the left.

Plate 208: A winter's morning in February, 1963 with one of the then new Swindon built Inter-City d.m.u. sets running through melting snow on the up main line in Sonning Cutting near Reading.

Plate 209: A British Rail Derby works built four car suburban set passes Dock Junction on the exit from St Pancras with the 14.10 all stations service to Luton on 25th March, 1975. The locomotive fuelling point can be seen to the rear of the train. Government approval has now been given to electrify this line as far as Bedford and on completion the reign of the diesel multiple units will be over.

Plate 210: On 21st September, 1976 the 16.37 Manchester to Rose Hill Marple train is captured approaching Romiley formed of two Gloucester Carriage & Wagon Company two car sets with Class 143 second driving trailer car No. M 56106 in front.

Plate 211: The scene at Abergavenny Monmouth Road station on 7th July, 1961, with a Swindon built three car cross country unit waiting patiently for the loading and unloading of parcels and mail to be completed. A plume of white smoke can be seen under the station footbridge, which is coming from a steam engine busily shunting parcels vans in the yard.

Plate 212: Refurnished British Rail Derby built two car unit formed of Class 108/1 car No's E 50638 and E 50637 departs from Skipton station with the 14.26 local service to Leeds on 24th September, 1976, whilst a Class 37 locomotive on a mixed freight moves slowly round the back of the station. A Class 31 locomotive idles in the bay platform coupled to a parcels van and ready for the next work of the day.

Plate 213: Amidst an urban background, two Craven twin units and a Derby built three car set form a local service to Royston on 22nd March, 1973, seen climbing Holloway bank, past Holloway South Down signal box on the right and the Up box by the former Motorail loading dock on the left. The Kings Cross outer suburban electrification is now well under way and overhead electric wires and colour light multi-aspect signalling is already in place in this locality.

Plate 214: Class 45 No. 45 067 steals from under the magnificent roof of St Pancras Station with the 13.05 service to Sheffield on 25th March, 1975. The seven platforms and ten roads in the station are covered by a 25,000 square foot glazed roof with an elliptical span 240 feet wide and 100 feet high. The structure is exceptionally light and elegant but also has great strength.

Class 45's

Plate 215: The 08.20 Birmingham to Plymouth service leaves Exeter (St Davids) on 13th July, 1976 behind Class 45 No. 45 112 *The Royal Army Ordnance Corps.* It rather looks as if the windscreen wiper blade on the secondman's side is about to fly into the air at any moment!

Class 45, 2500 bhp
1 Co Co 1

45 004 (77) *Royal Irish Fusilier*
45 006 (89) *Honourable Artillery Company*
45 014 (137) *The Cheshire Regiment*
45 022 (60) *Lytham St Annes*

45 023 (54) *The Royal Pioneer Corps*
45 039 (49) *The Manchester Regiment*
45 040 (50) *King's Shropshire Light Infantry*
45 041 (53) *Royal Tank Regiment*
45 043 (58) *The King's Own Royal Border Regiment*
45 044 (63) *Royal Inniskilling Fusilier*
45 045 (64) *Coldstream Guardsman*
45 046 (68) *Royal Fusilier*
45 048 (70) *The Royal Marines*
45 049 (71) *The Staffordshire Regiment (Prince of Wales's Own)*
45 055 (84) *Royal Corps of Transport*
45 059 (98) *Royal Engineer*
45 060 (100) *Sherwood Forester*
45 104 (59) *The Royal Warwickshire Fusilier*
45 111 (65) *Grenadier Guardsman*
45 112 (61) *The Royal Army Ordnance Corps*
45 118 (67) *The Royal Artilleryman*
45 123 (52) *The Lancashire Fusilier*
45 135 (99) *3rd Carabinier*
45 137 (56) *The Bedfordshire and Hertfordshire Regiment (T.A.)*
45 143 (62) *5th Royal Inniskilling Dragoon Guards*
45 144 (55) *Royal Signals*

Plate 216: No. 45 141 takes the through line at Nottingham (Midland) station with the 12.59 from Nottingham carriage sidings to Etches Park on 4th June, 1976 with empty coaching stock and parcels vans.

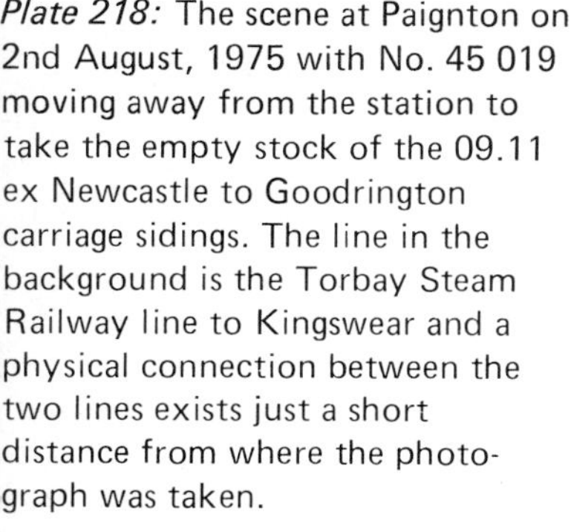

Plate 217: No. 45 072 crosses the lifting barrier style level crossing, controlled from the cabin over the line, at Barton Street just after leaving Gloucester Eastgate station with a cross country train bound for the West of England on a fine afternoon in July, 1975.

Plate 218: The scene at Paignton on 2nd August, 1975 with No. 45 019 moving away from the station to take the empty stock of the 09.11 ex Newcastle to Goodrington carriage sidings. The line in the background is the Torbay Steam Railway line to Kingswear and a physical connection between the two lines exists just a short distance from where the photograph was taken.

Plate 219: The 11.00 from Glasgow was the only timetabled southbound passenger service via Carlisle and Settle on Sunday 2nd August, 1976, hauled by No 45 073. The train is seen in late afternoon travelling under clear signals through Hellifield amidst a very pleasant moorland setting with farmhouse and outbuildings in evidence; no doubt a bleak and desolate scene in winter.

Plate 220: Class 45 locomotive No. 49 *The Manchester Regiment* (now renumbered 45 039) stands in Severn Tunnel Junction Station with the diverted 23.59 Glasgow to Bristol overnight service, complete with sleeping cars. The locomotive has just run round the train and is about to set off on the final leg of the journey on Sunday morning 14th July, 1974.

Plate 221: Class 45 locomotive No. 102 (since renumbered 45 140) powers the 09.20 Liverpool to Plymouth passenger service on 14th March, 1974, approaching Lansdown Junction, Cheltenham.

Plate 222: A block coal train from Toton meanders along between Bickley and St Mary Cray, a few yards from Chislehurst Junction on 28th August, 1974. Motive power is being provided by No. 45 130.

Plate 223: No. 45 129 negotiates the crossing at the north of Leicester station under cautionary semaphore signals on 4th June, 1976, at the head of the Leeds to St. Pancras Inter-City service. The Leicester North signal box can be clearly seen in the picture and the locomotive depot is to the right of the box.

In the Works

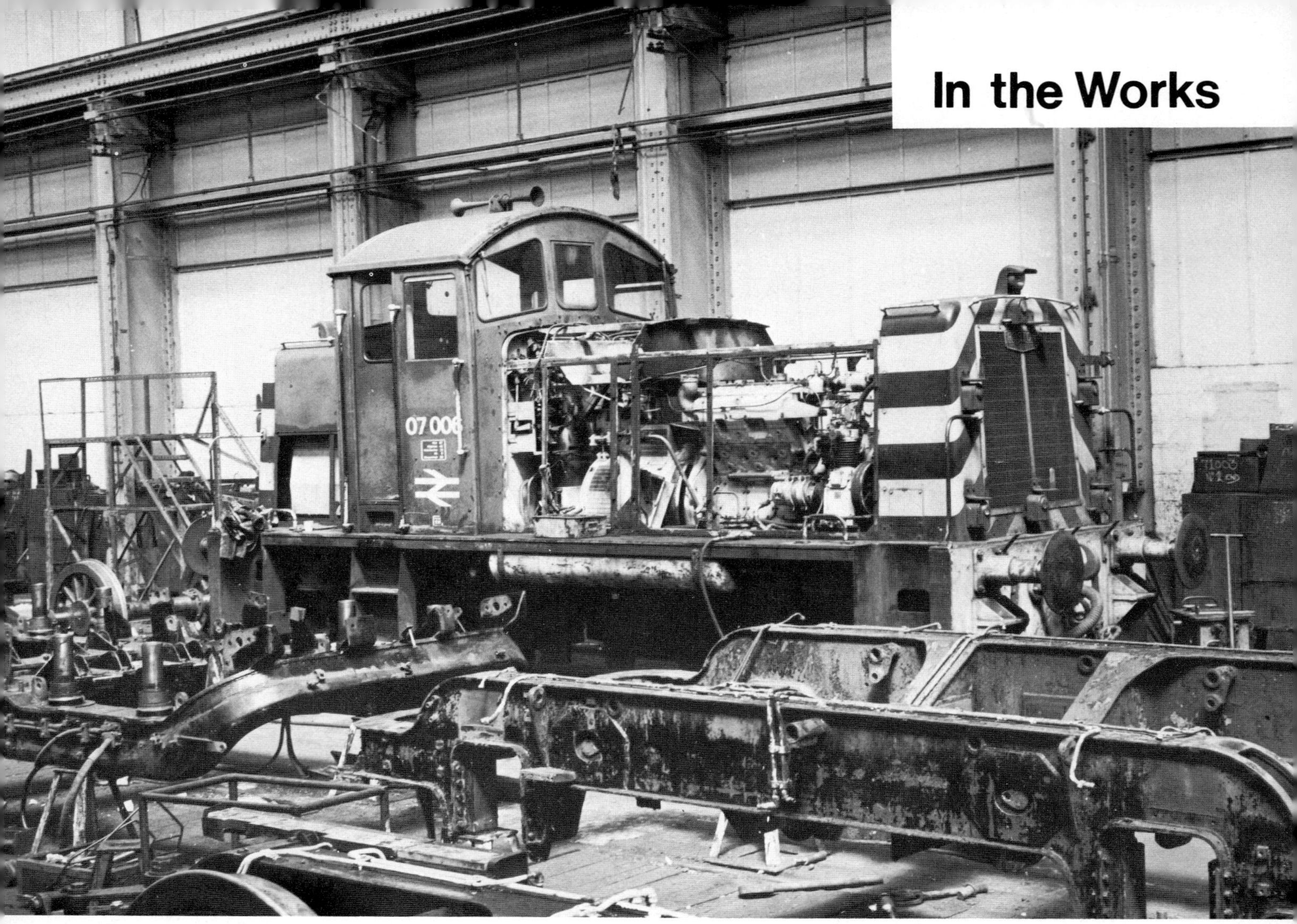

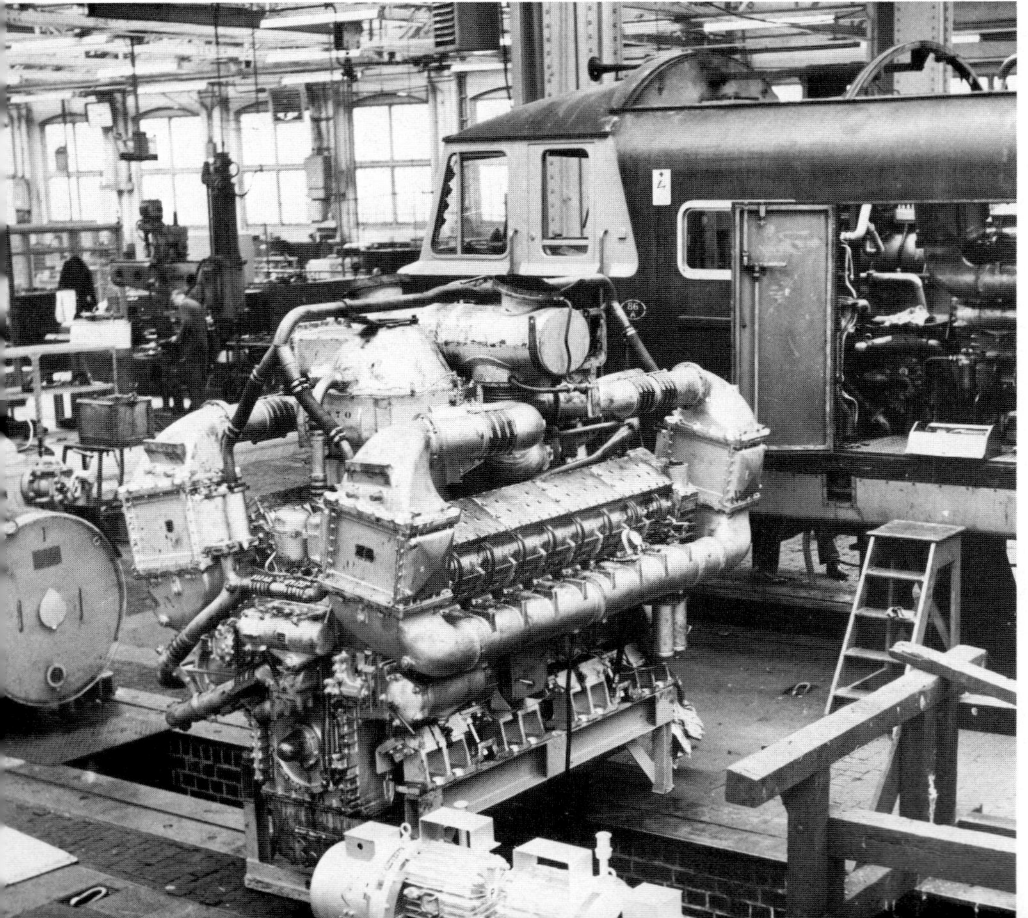

Plate 224: Class 07 Ruston & Hornsby 0-6-0 shunter No. 07 006 undergoes an overhaul inside Eastleigh works on 3rd May, 1976.

Plate 225: Inside Swindon Works, No. 5 Erecting Shop on 10th October, 1967. A Maybach type MD 870, 1750 bhp diesel engine is waiting to be installed in the Class 35 'Hymek' locomotive.

Plate 226: A demonstration for Swindon Works open day in 1968. 'Western' Class 52 locomotive No. D 1015 *Western Champion* in immaculate condition throughout, ready to be lifted back on its bogies in the Erecting Shop.

Plate 227: Bogie attention required. Brush Class 47 locomotive No. 47 409 is lifted and separated from its bogies at Sheffield Tinsley on 20th September, 1976.

Plate 228: Stripped right down for a major overhaul at Derby Works on 22nd November, 1975, is English Electric Bo-Bo Class 20 locomotive No. 20 003.

Class 46's

Plate 229: The only named Class 46 locomotive is No. 163 (now renumbered 46 026) *Leicestershire and Derbyshire Yeomanry,* photographed on 9th January, 1974 trundling along Lansdown loop, Cheltenham with a mixed freight train from Bescot to Severn Tunnel Junction.

Plate 230: The scene outside Dr. Day's Bridge Junction signal box, Bristol in February, 1970 with an Inter-City service headed by Class 46 locomotive No. 162, wending its way slowly past the box with part of the new track layout in the background.

Plate 231: Brake van travel for a party of rail enthusiasts on the 08.20 Severn Tunnel Junction to Ebbw Vale freight train on Saturday 10th May, 1975 hauled throughout by Class 46 locomotive No. 46 015; calling here at Waun-Lwyd (between Duffryn Yard and Cwm) for wagons to be attached on the return to Severn Tunnel Junction.

Plate 232: A Penzance to Bristol express hugs the coastline at Saltash on 19th September, 1976, headed by No. 46 004. An exceptionally pleasant stretch of track with water craft on one side and the apple orchards and gardens just across the railway line.

A look at Scotland

Plate 233: The line from Inverness — the capital of the Highlands — to Kyle of Lochalsh is 82¼ miles long and runs through some of the most attractive and mountainous areas of the British Isles. The line passes alongside lochs and over hills and moors inhabited by just a few sheep. On 6th June, 1973 Birmingham R.C. & W. Company type 2 Bo-Bo Class 26 locomotive No. 5341 (now renumbered 26 041) was the motive power provided for the 17.50 Kyle of Lochalsh to Inverness service. Here the train with parcel vans as well as passenger coaches crosses the moors and is just about to pass over a 'wee burn' near Achnasheen.

Plate 234: The same train calls at Achnasheen station, a lonely outpost of north west Scotland close to Loch a'Chroisg, but with little habitation nearby.

Plate 235: Things are fairly quiet at Pitlochry on 5th June, 1973, as a southbound engineers' train hauled by type 2 class 24 locomotive No. 5126 (later renumbered 24 126 and now withdrawn), discharges ballast for future track work.

Plate 236: Class 26 locomotive No. 5324 (now renumbered 26 024) enters Strathcarron station with the early evening train from Kyle of Lochalsh to Inverness on a summer's day in June, 1973. The single line train tablet is being held out of the side cab window ready to exchange with the one for the next station, whilst a gang of permanent way staff lay drainage pipes under the track.

Plate 237: The end of the line, with the Isle of Skye in the background just across the water from Kyle of Lochalsh. This picture was taken in the late afternoon on 22nd July, 1964, when the afternoon train for Inverness, with an unidentified Class 26 locomotive at its head, was making ready to leave and Class 24 No. D 5128 (later renumbered 24 128) was busy shunting in the yard. Both locomotives and coaching stock are in early BR livery.

Plate 238: Birmingham R.C. & W. Company type 2 Bo-Bo Class 27 No's. 5365 and 5379 arrive double heading a special train at the old Fort William terminus on 28th April, 1973. The locomotives and front coaches have pulled past the main station platforms, alongside the quay with the bus station behind. To allow for the town's by-pass construction, the 1894 built station was replaced with a new structure about half a mile south of this point; where the train is standing is now a dual carriageway by-pass road.

Plate 239: Three locomotives stand at the south end of Perth station on 20th July, 1964, all waiting for their next turns of duty. Class 24 No. 24 126 is in the foreground with Class 26 No's. 26 028 and 26 032 behind.

Plate 240: Ardlui is an important place on the Glasgow to Oban and Fort William line — it is one of the few passing points on what is otherwise single track. Here Class 27 locomotive No. 27 036, with score marks along the side, waits for the token from the approaching train before going forward into the next section.

Plate 241: Class 25 locomotive No. 5207 leaves the busy Aberdeen freight yard with the 12.50 freight train to Dundee on 6th November, 1973.

Plate 242: High up in the mountains Class 27 locomotive No. 5397 on the 10.05 Glasgow to Mallaig service pulls out of Crianlarich station and crosses the remaining short freight only section of the Callender and Oban route. A wood wagon is just visible in the sidings under the bridge — these are private sidings providing a great deal of log traffic for conveyance by rail to the pulp mills at Corpach.

Plate 243: The fast regular interval passenger service between Glasgow and Edinburgh is operated on a 'push pull' basis with locomotives at the front and rear of the train. This picture shows one of these trains passing through Princes Street Gardens on the approach to Edinburgh (Waverley) station with Class 27 locomotives front and rear on 21st February, 1975.

Plate 244: Two Birmingham R.C. & W Company type 2 Class 27 locomotives approach Mallaig junction just outside Fort William, double heading 1Z10, the return fourteen coach special train from London Euston run by the Midland & Great Northern Joint Railway Society. This was the first special charter train to use the newly opened Fort William station on 14th June, 1975.

Plate 245: Class 24 locomotive No. 5128 on the 10.50 train from Inverness to Wick and Thurso on 1st April, 1974, passing Clachnaharry just north of Inverness. An interesting operating feature on this line is that passenger trains are divided at Georgemas Junction, with one portion going to Wick and the other to Thurso.

Plate 246: The evening train from Kyle of Lochalsh to Inverness, worked by Class 25 No. 5341 nears its destination on a fine mid-summer evening in 1973, having joined the Highland main line at Dingwall. Although this line is now only single track, the bridge that the train is about to run over was built for double track.

Plate 247: Class 24 locomotives inside Ayr Motive Power Depot on the morning of 9th August, 1974.

Plate 248: Class 45 locomotive No. 53 (now renumbered 45 041) *Royal Tank Regiment* leaves Dumfries on 29th June, 1973 with a Leeds to Glasgow passenger service.

Plate 249: Class 20 locomotive No. 20 109 in Inverness depot yard on the evening of 9th August, 1974.

Plate 250: Class 27 locomotive No. 27 037 couples up to the empty stock off the 08.35 train from Glasgow (Queen Street) on 25th May, 1976, to await its next turn of duty. The famous McCaig's Tower overlooks the harbour and station. This circular coliseum like tower, built of granite, forms a unique back cloth to the attractive town of Oban.

Plate 251: Again at Oban on 25th May, 1976, this time soon after midday, No. 27 003 waits on the left with the 12.25 train to Glasgow (Queen Street) and on the right No. 27 037 takes a rest, whilst the railway staff chat about busier times!

Class 37's

Plate 252: Aberthaw in South Wales is an important loading point for pulverised flyash to be transported by rail. On 23rd June, 1970 a loaded train double headed by two Class 37 locomotives leaves the depot only minutes after another train of empty wagons has arrived.

Plate 253: Hardly worth all the effort in these days of locomotive shortages! English Electric type 3 Co-Co No. 37 041 speeds through Kensington Olympia with just two parcel vans on 24th March, 1976. Note the mixture of Western and Midland signals.

Plate 254: No 37 194 trundles along with a mixed freight train near Thirsk on 13th June, 1974.

Plate 255: The setting for this picture taken on 27th April, 1974 is Sonning Cutting on the London side of Reading. No. 37 012 passes by on the up main line with a train of empty double-deck car transporter wagons (Cartics).

Plate 256: The 1546 Inter-City service from Norwich to Liverpool Street begins its journey on 25th June, 1975 with No. 37 260 wending its way out of the East Anglian terminus which still boasts an interesting array of semaphore signals to control train movements.

Plate 257: Later the same afternoon No. 37 017 leaves Norwich with the 18.40 train to Liverpool Street The diesel multiple unit in the picture is taking fuel at the fuelling bay just outside the station.

The Latest 56's

Plate 258: A new class of locomotive is beginning to appear on British Rail metals — the Class 56 intermediate freight diesel-electric Co-Co's. The first batch of thirty are being built in Romania, towed across Europe and then over by train ferry from Zeebrugge to Harwich. The locomotives are rated as 3250 hp. weight 126 tons with a maximum speed of 80 mph; their design is based on the ubiquitous Brush 47 locomotive used extensively over BR. Sheffield Tinsley motive power depot has been active in testing and trying out the Class 56s. On 20th September, 1976 the line up in the depot included Class 20 No. 20 208, Class 56 No's. 56 002 and 56 005, and Class 31 No. 31 123.

Plate 259: A close up of Class 56 locomotive No. 56 001.

Plate 260: Another picture taken the same day at Sheffield Tinsley portrays No's. 56 005 and 56 003 at close quarters.

And so to the future?
Inter-City 125 High Speed Train

The Inter-City 125 High Speed Trains provide new standards of passenger comfort with much reduced journey times. Each train comprises two streamlined diesel-electric power cars, one at each end of the train and seven of the new 75 feet long Mark III passenger coaches including catering vehicles.

These trains are already in regular use on the Paddington — Bristol and South Wales services and they will soon be introduced on the East Coast main line for the services between Kings Cross and Edinburgh. On the latter route trains will have eight passenger coaches with the power cars having a slightly higher hp output in order that the 125 mph maximum speed and fast acceleration will equal those trains working on the Western Region.

Safety is obviously of prime importance and the disc brakes which are fitted to act on each wheel to ensure smooth and comfortable deceleration will enable the train to come to a stand from 125 mph within the existing stopping distances for 100 mph trains.

Plate 261: Bristol St Philips Marsh depot has been specially built for Inter-City 125 trains and deep wells are available to inspect the underneath of the trains without difficulty, as this picture clearly illustrates.

Plate 262: Platform No. 2 at Paddington on 6th October, 1976 — an Inter-City 125 service receives the 'right away' to commence its journey to Bristol.

Plate 263: Full line up of units at the well equipped Bristol St Philips Marsh High Speed Train depot. All the power cars and passenger coaches carry an individual fleet number on the side; in addition the power cars have a class and set number on the front i.e. Class 253 set 007. Two power cars carry the same unit number and should work together continually.

Plate 264: The inside of the driving cab of one of the Inter-City 125 power cars. This photograph was taken in the depot at Old Oak Common, near Paddington.

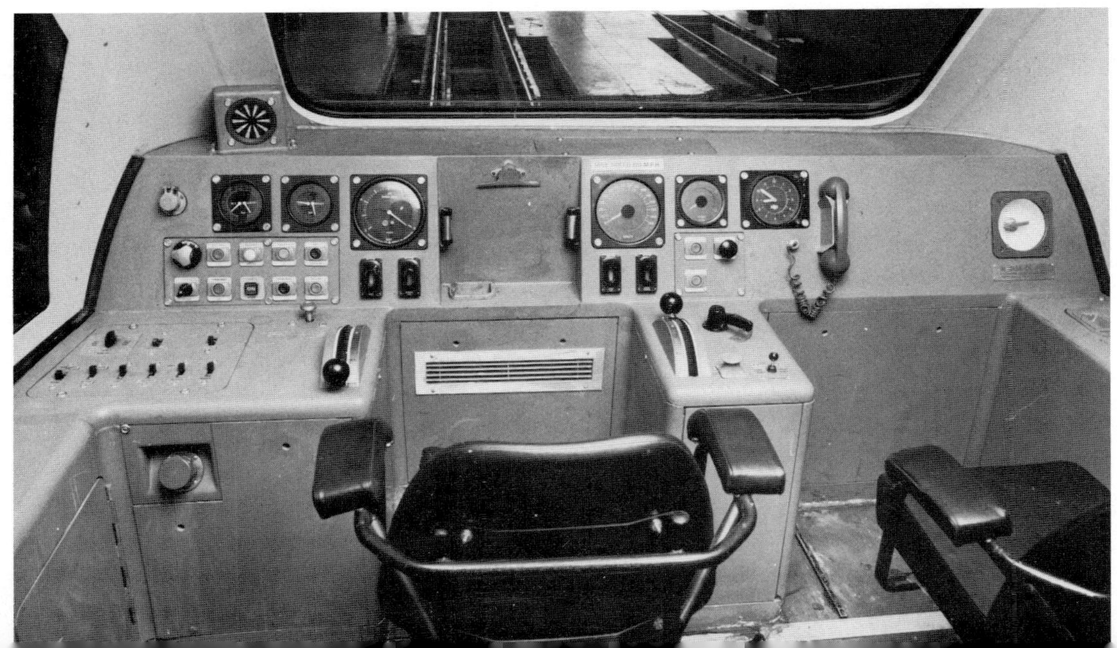

Plate 265: Standing alongside each other at Swindon station, British Rail's two record breaking trains. At the platform is the prototype High Speed Train which set a world speed record for diesel traction of 143 mph in June, 1973. On the through road is the experimental Advanced Passenger Train which became the fastest train ever to run in Britain when it achieved 152 mph on test in August, 1975.

OTHER NAMED LOCOMOTIVES

'Warship' Class
Diesel-Hydraulic Locomotives

D.600 *Active*
D.601 *Ark Royal*
D.602 *Bulldog*
D.603 *Conquest*
D.604 *Cossack*

D.800 *Sir Brian Robertson*
D.801 *Vanguard*
D.802 *Formidable*
D.803 *Albion*
D.804 *Avenger*
D.805 *Benbow*
D.806 *Cambrian*
D.807 *Caradoc*
D.808 *Centaur*
D.809 *Champion*
D.810 *Cockade*
D.811 *Daring*
D.812 *The Royal Naval Reserve 1859-1959*
D.813 *Diadem*
D.814 *Dragon*
D.815 *Druid*
D.816 *Eclipse*
D.817 *Foxhound*
D.818 *Glory*
D.819 *Goliath*
D.820 *Grenville*
D.821 *Greyhound*
D.822 *Hercules*
D.823 *Hermes*
D.824 *Highflyer*
D.825 *Intrepid*
D.826 *Jupiter*
D.827 *Kelly*
D.828 *Magnificent*
D.829 *Magpie*
D.830 *Majestic*

D.831 *Monarch*
D.832 *Onslaught*
D.833 *Panther*
D.834 *Pathfinder*
D.835 *Pegasus*
D.836 *Powerful*
D.837 *Ramillies*
D.838 *Rapid*
D.839 *Relentless*
D.840 *Resistance*
D.841 *Roebuck*
D.842 *Royal Oak*
D.843 *Sharpshooter*
D.844 *Spartan*
D.845 *Sprightly*
D.846 *Steadfast*
D.847 *Strongbow*
D.848 *Sultan*
D.849 *Superb*
D.850 *Swift*
D.851 *Temeraire*
D.852 *Tenacious*
D.853 *Thruster*
D.854 *Tiger*
D.855 *Triumph*
D.856 *Trojan*
D.857 *Undaunted*
D.858 *Valorous*
D.859 *Vanquisher*
D.860 *Victorious*
D.861 *Vigilant*
D.862 *Viking*
D.863 *Warrior*
D.864 *Zambesi*
D.865 *Zealous*
D.866 *Zebra*
D.867 *Zenith*
D.868 *Zephyr*
D.869 *Zest*
D.870 *Zulu*

English Electric, class 40
2000 bhp 1 Co Co 1

40 010 (210) *Empress of Britain*
40 011 (211) *Mauretania*
40 012 (212) *Aureol*
40 013 (213) *Andania*
40 014 (214) *Antonia*
40 015 (215) *Aquitania*
40 016 (216) *Campania*
40 017 (217) *Carinthia*
40 018 (218) *Carmania*
40 019 (219) *Caronia*
40 020 (220) *Franconia*
40 021 (221) *Ivernia*
40 022 (222) *Laconia*
40 023 (223) *Lancastria*
40 024 (224) *Lucania*
40 025 (225) *Lusitania*
40 027 (227) *Parthia*
40 028 (228) *Samaria*
40 029 (229) *Saxonia*
40 030 (230) *Scythia*
40 031 (231) *Sylvania*
40 032 (232) *Empress of Canada*
40 033 (233) *Empress of England*
40 034 (234) *Accra*
40 035 (235) *Apapa*